TRiVjUM

The mark of perseverance

Trivium

the mark of perseverance

JOE SHOOMAN

Independent Music Press

Published in 2006 by
INDEPENDENT MUSIC PRESS
Independent Music Press is an imprint of I.M. P. Publishing Limited
This Work is Copyright © I. M. P. Publishing Ltd 2006

Trivium: The Mark Of Perseverance by Joe Shooman

British Library Cataloguing-in-Publication Data.
A catalogue for this book is available from The British Library.
ISBN: 0-9552822-0-9 and 978-0-9552822-0-1

Cover Design by Fresh Lemon.
Edited by Martin Roach.

Printed in the UK.

Independent Music Press
P.O. Box 69,
Church Stretton, Shropshire
SY6 6WZ

Visit us on the web at: www.impbooks.com

For a free catalogue, e-mail us at: info@impbooks.com
Fax: 01694 720049

contents

acknowledgements

Rock 'n' roll thanks to all who kindly gave up their time to be interviewed for this book. Metaphorical bottles of JD are due, in alphabetical order, to Jarred Bonaparte, Ritchie Brown, Toby 'Ikki' Brown, Gizz Butt, Yuka Hirose, Bradley Lewter, Stefan Luedicke, 'Hardcore' George Moore, Mike Poggione, Dale 'Rage' Resteghini, Colin Richardson, Josh Rothstein, Mark Sutherland, Alex 'Ronaldinho' Vieira and Orlando Metal Awards guru, Matt Wagner.

For their input, suggestions, help and supreme support way beyond the call of duty, absinth-tinged wickedness is directed toward Andy Daley, Bob Deutsch @ Prosthetic Records, Jason Ferguson, Jon Hall and all @ Spank Records, Mike Hanson, Jeff 'DIY' Hogan, Johnny K, Will Kinsman and Niall Doherty @ The Fly, Dan Morris @ Satan's FishTank, Isac Nordgren, Raziq Rauf, Nick Tesco, Karen Toftera, Carlton Wuck and SW.

In making it happen at all, studded wristbands the size of small countries are due to Jake Kennedy and Joel McIver, Mart, and Rodney Hughes, who rocked harder than anyone else and in more ways than people realised.

Unimaginable thanks and love to Mam and Dad for everything.

Everything for Zoë.

To absent friends Mark, Tecwyn, Johnny and Oz: rockin' out up above.

Joe Shooman, July 14, 2006.

I

some facts

Orlando, a city smack in the middle of Orange County, Florida, is home to the original Disneyworld. Orlando was either named after a character in Shakespeare's As You Like It, or for a fallen scout in the Seminole Wars, Sentinel Orlando Reeves. Its initial 1874 population of just 85 has now stabilised at just under two hundred thousand inhabitants.

These are facts.

The sort of things that you learn at school.

More facts.

Forty kilometres north of Orlando lies a small and somewhat unassuming workers' city by the name of Altamonte Springs. Its population is just shy of forty two thousand. Many people commute to Orlando itself, day on day, to feed the slavering maw of industry. They raise families in Altamonte Springs with the proceeds of their efforts. If you are a kid, growing up in Altamonte Springs, chances are that you'll end up at Lake Brantley High School.

At Lake Brantley High, you will learn other facts. Facts concerning certain former inmates (also known as 'students') of the institution. Students who have made Lake Brantley High, Altamonte Springs and Orlando itself famous worldwide. You will not learn about these students – yet – from the core curriculum at school. But you will hear of them on the radio. You will see their logo on T-shirts. You will see their faces and watch them growl with passion and electric-blooded effervescence on MTV. You will read their thoughts in magazines.

These former students are part of a musical group. A musical group who have sold hundreds of thousands of records throughout the world.

The most important fact you will learn is this: this musical group is, arguably, the greatest force in Heavy Metal since Metallica.

The group is called Trivium.

"My first dream was to be a truck driver."

For Travis Smith, life was all about music. It more or less always had been, as he told Dan Morris of *Satan's Fish Tank* 'zine. "My first dream was to be a truck driver," he said, "and then I found out my dad wanted me to play guitar – I tried it for a little bit but I can't play for shit!"[1]

He did, however, find his niche instrument pretty quickly, telling *Drummer Magazine*'s Owen Hopkin, "I got into drumming [also] through my dad, a really big music fan and I remember growing up listening to his Eagles,

Tom Petty and Lynyrd Skynyrd records. I would put up a practice kit made out of pots and pans from the kitchen and play along to the music he was playing."[2] "I would have rubber bands and I would take the lids and hang the lids from the rubber bands so I had like cymbals hanging."[3]

"I realized I wanted to beat the shit out of things. I wanna pound the fuck out of some drums."

Born in Bainbridge, Georgia (population 11,772, fact fans) on April 29, 1982, Travis had decided at a very early age that the insistent rhythms flying and fizzing within him would form and define his career. "I've always loved music and I love playin' it," he said. "I think I was about five years old when it first clicked in my mind that I wanted to do this for the rest of my life."[4] "I realized I wanted to beat the shit out of things. I wanna pound the fuck out of some drums."[5]

Subsequently, the drummer's supportive parents paid for seven years of lessons, during which he learnt technique, music theory, a wider appreciation of music including jazz, before his drum teacher suggested that Travis play along with records he liked. "I remember bringing in *Nevermind* [Nirvana], *And Justice For All* [Metallica], *Rust In Peace* [Megadeth] and *Cowboys From Hell* [Pantera]," he continued, "sounds that I was really into, drummers that I thought were great and people I really wanted to play like. It was cool to go in there and learn what I wanted to learn. A lot of teachers basically just wanted to teach you what's out of the book and that gets really boring."[6]

Travis found himself more than ready to take these lessons into a wider sphere. It was time to get out there, find some like-minded musicians, and show the world what they could do... and where it really mattered: onstage. An opportunity to do just that soon presented itself with Teague Middle School's regular Battle Of The Bands competition. Playing at that contest was an act put together by Brad Lewter – from one point of view, the first incarnation of Trivium.

"It really started with [another friend] Jarred Bonaparte and myself," Lewter told this author in an exclusive conversation for this book. "We had been friends since elementary school and developed a taste for distortion and loud volumes in middle school. We jammed regularly and played 'Smells Like Teen Spirit' at the Battle Of The Bands show. The line-up for that was myself on guitar and vocals, Jarred on guitar, Matt Schuler on guitar, Ryan Selis on bass, and Eyal Bar on drums."

"Travis, who was a year ahead of us, saw the show and got in contact with Jarred and me," continues Lewter, "he wanted to put something together to play the Battle Of The Bands at Lake Brantley High School which we would be attending within months. Jarred and I began jamming with Travis at his house and began leaning towards a heavier sound to accommodate Travis's machine gun double bass."

"At first, we exclusively played Nirvana covers and simply rocked out," remembers Bonaparte, when I asked him about those early days. "When we got a little serious – although we were never that serious – we parted ways with our bassist and I switched to [that instrument]."

"I remember Travis would sit in front of the TV with just his bass drum and double pedal, playing runs for hours," laughs Lewter, "but we didn't have a name to enter the Battle under, so I spent days with Roget's running names by my mother and sister."

"I was looking for something that described our (then) three-piece in a decidedly metal fashion. We settled on

Trivium, as its root was Latin for the convergence of three roads. I found it was also the term for the three foundational studies in medieval schooling, consisting of grammar, logic, and rhetoric. Jarred and Travis seemed to like the name, so we went with it."

Whilst Travis – who'd previously jammed with a long-forgotten act called Petl – was making his first forays into a structured band set-up, across town a Navy kid was studiously practicing his guitar licks, hour on hour, in his bedroom, staring at the posters of his geetar heroes on his walls or watching Metallica's live 1989 Seattle Coliseum gig on video over and over again, determined that one day he himself would attain such heights.

Matthew Kiichi Heafy was born in Iwakuni, Japan on January 26, 1986 – the year Metallica released their *Master Of Puppets* album. His US Navy father, Brian Heafy, was stationed in Iwakuni, a heavy-industry fixated Japanese city, and had married a local lass, Yoshiko. Brian's job necessitated an itinerant lifestyle – after a year in Iwakuni, the family had moved around the US for the best part of a decade with pit stops at California, Florida and Arlington Heights, Illinois before finally settling down in Altamonte Springs when Matt was in fifth grade.

"When I was eleven or twelve I was into radio rock and punk," Matt said, "I wanted to play guitar because it looked cool, but I sucked really, really bad. I tried out for a band but I got kicked out because I couldn't play a punk song."[7] To un-suck his playing, he subsequently took lessons for around three-and-a-half years with Dave Hopwood, a member of the band October.

Matt and Travis had, in fact, first met as band mates – of sorts – whilst both at Lake Brantley, as classmate George Moore explained when I asked him about those formative days. "We were actually all in a marching band together, if you can believe that. Matt played saxophone and I played trumpet. Travis was in the marching band too, but I didn't talk to him cause he was a senior."

"The reason Matt and I met was that people were really impressed by the fact that I could tap on guitar," he laughs, "and people were like, 'Whoa, dude, you're shredding on guitar! Dude, Matt Heafy knows how to do that; you should have a guitar showdown'. It was funny: I was into hardcore back then so my nickname round school was Hardcore George. Heafy was really heavy into Metallica so they were calling him Metal Matt Heafy! It was Metal Matt vs Hardcore George. It was really funny; it was like a stupid high school thing."

"As we prepared for the Battle, we found that we lacked the wicked shredding lead that metal demands," continues Brad Lewter, "Matt Schuler was still a good friend but detested metal entirely. His younger brother Drew, however, quite enjoyed the genre and his best friend at the time was a young and talented guitarist by the name of Matt Heafy."

"I played in a talent show when I was thirteen, in the eighth grade, and the original singer of Trivium heard me," Matt Heafy recalled, "then he brought me over to the drummer's house and had me try out. Everybody else was seventeen, eighteen: I was thirteen. They were all really confused about it, but as soon as I started playing, their opinion changed. They were like, 'Okay, this guy's in.'"[8]

Travis laughs at the memory. "We were going to be doing Metallica covers and Matt's name came up. We jammed on 'For Whom The Bell Tolls' and it sounded great, so I knew this was the guy that we were going to have."[9] "He was so young at the time, and it was awesome. I knew right then that there was something special about him."[10]

The two hit it off straight away when they realised they shared an ambition – or a dream. "After [the successful try-out] we got talking about Metallica and I told [Travis] my personal goal was to be in a band that is going to be the next Metallica," Matt told *Metal Hammer*, "and, funnily enough, that was his goal too."[11]

A journey in the passenger seat of Travis' battered-up car, travelling back from a marching band rehearsal, also proved to be something of a road-to-Damascus moment. The drummer slipped a battered and well-worn cassette copy of Megadeth's *Rust In Peace* into his stereo, and explosions went off in Heafy's head.

"I had only listened to pop-punk and nu-metal before that," he explained to Jon Wiederhorn of *Guitar World* magazine, "there I was, sweating my ass off in 95 degree weather with no air-conditioning, and this music came on Travis' stereo. It was so heavy, and so technical. That hooked me onto thrash metal."[12]

"The sound seemed to coalesce with Matt's lead," continues Lewter. "We entered the Battle Of The Bands playing a few covers and an original. Matt was allowed to play, as the majority of the band attended Lake Brantley. I remember we covered Tool's 'Stinkfist' and Metallica's 'For Whom The Bell Tolls', with a break into 'One'. The crowd seemed pleased, but the judges went with some God-rock for the win!"

"We took the crowd response as a good sign and continued to practice writing some new originals, and wrote an early version of 'Fugue' called 'Toccata And Fugue'. We worked on getting some gigs and played a couple of parties. The first party we played was at the house of my now-fiancée – where we had our first run-in with the police because of noise!"

"Travis signed us up for an Orlando city-wide Battle Of The Bands," recalls Lewter, "and we placed second to a seasoned band of twenty-somethings – not bad for having no member over sixteen. Following that show, Matt's father Brian started getting a lot more serious. I remember coming to a practice to find that he had legally copyrighted the name."

The writing was on the wall for Brad, whose leanings toward art and computer animation – plus his musical predilections – were becoming untenable with the growing metallic sound of Trivium.

"Listening to a lot of the Melvins and Tool, I began pushing for a more prog/math rock sound," concludes Lewter, "while Matt insisted on old school thrash *à la* Metallica. I was getting serious about art as well, so the decision to leave was only logical."[13]

"The three of us, excluding the original singer, were all heavily into Metallica, Megadeth and Pantera," Matt told *Pit Magazine*, "He wasn't!"[14] As Travis says, "He ended up parting ways with us because he wanted to do different kinds of music. We were like 'Fuck that, we wanna play fuckin' metal.' He left the band and we just kept the fuckin' name. It was creative differences."[15] Ah, that old chestnut.

"We want people to feel like they're a part of us – which they are."

The problems engendered by being a band with plenty of ambition but no, uh, singer were swiftly sidestepped by one of Travis's more inspired decisions. In a moment of laser-clear genius, he found himself marching round to the Heafy residence and press-ganging the young guitarist into action. "I remember walking up to his house and knocking on the door and saying 'Dude, you're going to be the new singer,'" Smith told Jordan McLachlan of *Rhythm Magazine*. "He wasn't feeling it at first – he didn't think he could sing or anything. But it came; he just worked on it and we got there. I knew how he used his time, how he used to work on his guitar playing, and I knew he'd do the same for his vocals. So that's what I saw in him. That made me think it would work – and it did."[16]

Well, eventually anyway. To put it delicately, Heafy's age meant he wasn't fully developed in more ways than one. "I couldn't sing," he laughed, "I was still going through puberty! But everything worked out. After school I would play along to [the album] *Master Of Puppets* every day. I would sing and play guitar."[17]

"I was, like, '[James Hetfield] is the perfect person who's gonna lead you by example,'" Travis told *Rock Sound*, "'Watch Hetfield, that's the man you wanna be like. He is so energetic, he is so cool with the crowd, and he just gives you this awesome feeling, and that's what we want too when we're at shows – we want people to feel like they're a part of us – which they are.'"[18]

"The early gigs were mostly birthday parties and we played covers of whatever was popular – Korn, Deftones, Slipknot," recalls Jarred. "Our big thing was Battles, we played every one we could find. Never won though."

Adding second guitarist Brent Young – who'd jammed with Travis in previous incarnations – to the line-up shortly afterwards, the four-piece set about some hard rehearsing. Matt's ever-supportive pop, Brian (who'd played in various bands over the years as a guitarist) was now managing the group.

Another fact. Orlando, in 2000, boasted the rarest of things: a venue which was actually prepared to give young bands a chance to play. It was the legendary DIY Venue, also known during the day as Jeff Hogan's tiny punk rock music store, DIY Records. Toby 'Ikki' Brown was responsible for booking gigs. "It was primarily a punk/indie-rock/hardcore music venue," he explained to this author. "The crowds would range from five kids, to being packed in like sardines. I remember booking

Trivium at DIY. I had never booked them before, but they were requesting a show and I was happy to help them out. I remember thinking they were pretty good and giving them a few opening slots with different bands."

That debut DIY show may not have been the most high-profile of starts, but it was in many ways a pivotal moment. Also on the bill were local black metal act Mindscar, the brainchild of guitarist Ritchie Brown. He has fond memories of rapping backstage with Heafy at that concert: "I think I asked him what guitar players he liked and he said, 'Van Halen!' and I said, 'Van Halen SUCKS!' And he was like, 'You're an asshole.' And then we became friends!"

"At the time I met Matt, he was really into Metallica, straight metal. That's what Trivium sounded like, and Mindscar sounded European. We had stuff that sounded like At The Gates or In Flames."

Not long after Trivium's appearances at DIY, the venue sadly shut down, and Orlando lost another ground-level contact with the raft of talent searching to break through.

Trivium were also finding it kinda difficult to break through into the main Orlando venues, so Matt Heafy's new buddy offered him a deal that would benefit both parties. "Trivium weren't playing concerts, and Mindscar was already playing concerts in Orlando," recalls Ritchie Brown. "At the time, one of my friends, Dan Lehmann, who liked Iron Maiden a lot, wanted to record some stuff. And we made a deal that Matt would record my friend's band cause he had a little 8-track, and in return I'd book him some shows with Mindscar."

The shows may have been growing in number, but Trivium was to require another tweak to their line-up. It had been fun so far, but the bassist was running into a tricky spell.

"Travis is the best damn drummer ever. Period," Bonaparte says. "Him, Brent and I used to hang out all the time and have fun. Brent's the funniest motherfucker ever, and he was an awesome guitarist. The three of us had a lot of fun. Matt and I started out as really good friends, and we would hang out all the time when we weren't rehearsing. However, Travis, Brent and I picked on him a lot and made fun of him – and it began to piss him off which I'm sure was the reason for my demise. That kid at twelve was a great guitarist; at fourteen was the best guitarist I knew; and now he fucking rocks! The only issue is that he knew this at twelve!"

"I left the band in my senior year of high school," remembers Bonaparte, "because my parents basically said either go to college or get out of the house when you graduate. Brent and Travis say the night that I left the band it was never meant to happen like it did, instead they were going to ask me to step up for more practicing or phase someone else in, but instead it ended abruptly."

"So I started playing bass," says Ritchie Brown. "It wasn't like I joined Trivium as a creative mind – it was more like they were my friends and they needed a bass player, and I was helping them."

Travis, Matt, Brent and Ritchie started hitting the Orlando circuit – such as it was – cutting their gig teeth at a succession of venues. "We were playing at the Lost & Found, and a place called the Fairbanks Inn – the FBI," recalls Brown. "Those were the main gig places for bands starting out at that time." The Trivium set at this point mostly comprised of fairly obvious cover versions, including Megadeth, Korn and Marilyn Manson, as 'Hardcore George' Moore recalls. "Matt had long hair and they'd just play Metallica *Black Album*-style and wear black tank tops, headbanging, putting up the horns and all that shit. It was kinda great."

During mid-2001, the band reshuffled their line-up once again; after a certain amount of looking for a new bassist to replace Brown, one day guitarist Brent Young solved the problem internally by picking up the boom-boom four-stringer in rehearsal. Serendipitously he turned out to be a naturally adept player.

Brown had left Trivium amicably to concentrate on his main project, Mindscar, who at the time were making some waves in Orlando – and beyond. The ambitious Matt Heafy actually momentarily joined that black metal act as a guitarist. "We were having a lot of fun with Mindscar after I stopped playing bass for Trivium," recalls Brown, "so me and Matt concentrated on Mindscar together and put Trivium on hold." However, according to Brown it all fell apart on the eve of a major national tour, when Mindscar suffered personnel problems and lost a drummer.

"We had a concert coming up, and Matt still played all the chords with three fingers!"

So it could all have been such a different story. You may not now be learning of Trivium from the TV, from magazines, from T-shirts and from radio. You would not be reading this book. In fact, there's another reason that you might not be learning of Trivium at all, thanks to that drummer again, who almost put Heafy out of action permanently.

"We used to have little boxing sessions at our practice, cause we liked to have a bunch of fun," continues Brown. "[Mindscar's] drummer, Mike Radford, broke Matt's finger – I think it was his pinky! And he had to go to the hospital." Luckily, however, Heafy's growing mastery of his instrument carried him through it. "We had a concert coming up, and Matt still played all the chords with three fingers!"

When Mindscar fell to pieces, Heafy focussed again on his main band; not wanting to throw away the creative relationship he'd developed with Brown, however, he offered the guitarist a place in Trivium. "They always wanted me to play lead guitar," muses Ritchie. "I always wanted to but I felt like the other guys in Mindscar were my original friends from when I was a kid, and I felt torn between two places. So I kinda stuck with my original friends – who ended up [parting ways with] me anyway! Now I'm doing more of what I wanna do, as are they, so everybody's happy and we're all still friends."

It was the beginning of something that would turn out to be very special. Something that, one day, may yet be legendary. Something that grew from talent shows and hobby bands at Lake Brantley High School, something that shows no signs of being stilled.

That something was a musical group called Trivium, and they were up and running.

ב

Metal Rewards

Matt Wagner grew up in Leesburg (population: who cares), a town an hour north of Orlando. Obsessed with heavy music, and a member of the group 5 Billion Dead, he moved to a Big City full of undeniably talented musicians. But it was also a city rife with undue, surly competition and snide remarks between fractious fragmented stylistic ghettos, formed by people who really should have been working together for the good of all, as he explained to me exclusively for this book.

"What I was finding was that the guys who liked, for example, extreme metal were very unsupportive and very snobbish," Wagner says, shaking his head sadly. "If it wasn't extreme metal they wouldn't support it, they'd say 'They SUCK!' But even if this was, say, a nu-metal band, they're still playing the same venues; they're still going through the same struggles; they still have to lug their equipment onstage, just like everyone else. We're all in this together."

The solution? Set up the Orlando Metal Awards, and try and bring the diverse and often warring factions toward some sort of common ground. "I modelled the Orlando Metal Awards after the Tampa Bay Metal Awards," continues Wagner. "It was very successful down there. We had a lot of people here who were into the metal scene, but there really wasn't a lot of unity. So I put together the Orlando Metal Awards to try and unify the scene, kinda bring the bands together, bring the fans together, and I'm glad to say that it was a legendary success!"

To make an awards show happen, of course, you're gonna need a pretty damn fine line-up to play live on the night. Wagner set about taking in as many local gigs as he possibly could, which inevitably meant rubbing shoulders with Trivium. But when he first caught them at a Lake Brantley gig, he wasn't so impressed. "I'd heard about them," he recalls, "and they were playing their local high school talent show – that was like their first gig together. It was quite amazing. Soon after that I saw them at a little nightclub called Lost & Found. Trivium had been coming in for a very long time to ask for a gig, and the venue finally gave in and let them play a coupla songs. And, to be honest with you, they were pretty horrible – they were terrible! They played some really bad covers of Metallica songs: 'For Whom The Bell Tolls', and I think 'Whiplash'. They didn't have a lot of material."

"I had noticed that even though they were playing these Metallica covers, Matt was a pretty good guitar player," says Wagner. "At the time, he was really concentrating on learning – and Metallica was his favourite band, so he had a good teacher in Kirk Hammett to study and get his chops down."

Alex Vieira, a band mate of Wagner in 5 Billion Dead, also caught Trivium, this time at Indiefest, and he was impressed by their professionalism. "It was outside, there was a really small stage and a small PA," explained Vieira to the author, "they were one of the very few heavy bands who were part of that competition. It was really interesting; when they showed up you could tell the difference. They had a look: 'OK, those guys are definitely in a band', as compared to all the other bands who didn't look like they were doing it seriously. Just like, 'Let's put a band together for the weekend, play the Battle Of The Bands and that's it'."

"Trivium, you gotta check them out — they're really young but they're really good!"

"When you attend a high school battle, usually the equipment is not at a professional level; they're beginners, they're just getting their stuff together. The kids show up with their guitars, their combo amps and a few pedals here and there. Trivium showed up and Matt had a full Marshall stack! He was playing a Les Paul, and a Dimebag signature guitar! They all dressed the part, you know, in black clothes. At the time, they looked more like a Death Metal band than anything else."

"That was the only thing anyone talked about," Vieira continues, "'Trivium, you gotta check them out — they're really young but they're really good!' I was watching them and I was like 'Wow!' There was so much energy coming from them. It was amazing. You don't see that every day! I was going to shows all the time to see local bands play and there was nothing quite that intense going on at the time."

Matt Wagner followed Trivium's progress thereafter with some interest, and noticed that over the period 2000-

2001, the band begun to solidify into a battle-hardened unit. "Eventually, Trivium started making a little bit more of a buzz for themselves," he continues, "and I saw them play probably two more times after that first gig. And then, next thing you know it's like 'Holy Crap! These guys are pretty good!' So I gave Matt and Trivium a shot to play at this club. And they were a huge hit that day; they had developed a really good following because all their high school friends had come out. Trivium always credit me for giving them their first break in terms of a big show in front of a large crowd."

Buzzing from their live breakthrough, and now rapidly becoming a tight-as-hell outfit, Trivium proceeded to lay some tracks to tape for the first time. The three-song demo – never available to the general public as such – comprises the inevitable cover of 'For Whom The Bell Tolls' alongside two original compositions; the doomy 'Pain' – soaked in melodic feedback and lo-slung, chug-riffing – and the epic, seven minute 'Thrust'. The quality of recording's muddy as hell, the drums sound like Travis has reverted to the snaffled kitchenware pot 'n' pan 'kit' upon which he started thrashing about as a five-year-old, and the singing – to put it mildly – isn't quite as powerful as Hetfield, Matt sounding like a constipated cookie monster. But all the elements are there: searching, soaring guitar licks, rampant double-bass-pedal action, the fast-moving riffs, the dark-chord chuggles and contrasting middle eights. It is, recognisably, Trivium. Bearing in mind that songwriter Heafy was only just fifteen years of age at the time, it's a remarkable first foray with musicianship that not only outshreds groups many years their senior, but is an incredibly powerful portent of what was to come. All this coming from a kid who was spending his days stuck behind a grubby school desk reading up on classic literature, and daydreaming.

"I remember enjoying it when we read *Hamlet* and *Romeo And Juliet*. I really like Shakespeare's stuff," he mused, "but not enough to read on leisure time. Just in school it was alright. I don't pay attention in classes, I just think about songs, tab them, and write lyrics. I usually write it all out in tabulature in school."[19]

Outside Lake Brantley's frustrating – but enlightening – confines, the band was starting to make a real name for themselves at a local level, as Alex Vieira recalls. "Going to school full-time, and having a band on the side, and playing gigs on the weekend – Trivium did their fair share of playing concerts around here. It's hard to play a lot of shows in a local market that's saturated with bands, cause after a few shows pretty much everyone in the local scene knows who you are. If you don't have anything new to offer, the shows will be like, 'Ow! Those guys are playing again. I saw them last week, I'm not going again.' But as far as getting their name out in the local scene – everybody knew who they were."

The raising of awareness as to the band's activities was largely down to the influence of Brian Heafy. Up until that point, the group had hardly needed the guidance and skill of a manager, but as people started to prick up their ears, Brian began to ramp up the promotional activities in earnest.

"Brian was doing a lot of the promoting. Matt didn't do much except write songs and eat a lot of subs – then he went to the gym a lot," says 'Hardcore George'. "Brian is cool, he's a no-bullshit kinda guy. He is really charismatic, a fun guy to be around. But when it comes down to business, like anybody who knows their stuff, he's not afraid to be an asshole. You gotta be that way." Toby Brown of Ikky Promotions remembers dealing with Brian at early DIY Venue bookings with fondness. "He was *way* into them," he recalls, "best dad support I've ever seen."

Mindscar's Ritchie Brown also has good memories of Heafy the elder. "He's probably one of my favourite people in the whole world," offers the guitarist, "he's the coolest father anyone could ever have, and the most supportive person ever. He completely supported them financially, the business side, everything – his support is really, really, definitely one of the key ingredients to Trivium's success. Without it I don't think they'd be where they are today because they wouldn't have had so many opportunities." Alex Vieira agrees. "I have very good things to say about Brian, he's a great guy," he says, "of course, he's always looking after Trivium's best interests. Always. His kid's in the band."

"The two of them have more of an older guy to younger guy friendship, rather than just father and son. When you see the two of them hanging out it's like they're really good friends. He never imposes his 'father' image when he's dealing with Matt and fans and people around the band. You can tell that there's a businessman and a friend before you see the father. Only people who are really close to him, I guess, get to see that side."

"I couldn't have told you then that Trivium were gonna be the 'Next Big Thing'."

For now, aside from some serious flyering and a growing word-of-mouth buzz, the business side would be secondary to the continuing development of Trivium as a feasible three-piece band, and to that end the group stepped up activity a touch with more appearances at Lost & Found and the FBI, till once more the 2002 Orlando Metal Awards loomed.

Memorial Weekend, May 15, was a moment to savour for everyone who saw Matt Heafy pick up the award for

'Best Lead Guitarist'. Brilliantly, Matt wasn't there to pick it up, as OMA guru Matt Wagner explains. "He didn't think he was going to win," Wagner laughs, "and he was actually in the car on the way home from the gig! He thought there was no way he was gonna win this award. So I looked like a dumbass standing onstage with the trophy! I think I gave it to his dad, because he was still hanging around partying with us, and Brian called Matt up on his cell-phone, and he just flipped out and screamed: 'NO WAYYY!'"

"I couldn't have told you then that Trivium were gonna be the 'Next Big Thing'. But I could have told you then that Matt was going to be 'A Star'. He was good enough that he didn't have to be the frontman of a band to outshine the other people. He could be in just about any band that he wants to be in, and play any style of music that he wanted to play – because he was determined to be an accomplished musician. Most kids that age don't know what they're doing; he was seventeen when he won the 'Best Lead Guitar Player' in Orlando. And this is not a small city! There's a lot of musicians here, you know. For a seventeen year old to be better than most of the adults is a pretty amazing thing."

Trivium, now complete with 'Award Winning Guitarist', had also started to snag a few snazzy support slots with touring bands visiting Orlando. The youngsters weren't overawed by appearances alongside national acts including the soon-to-be-defunct Pissing Razors, of El Paso (interesting fact: Pissing Razors' first incarnation, Sadist, broke up when the original singer joined the US Navy.) Nor were Trivium shiny-eyed, frozen or despondent as they rocked the house as first act on October 13, 2002's gig at The Haven, playing in a strong bill that also featured Mindscar, Aruspex and Reflux. It was a gig headlined by Baltimore's 'dungeon metal' scoundrels

Pessimist – whose constant line-up changes put Trivium's own early reshuffles firmly to shame.

Another jaunt to a local studio in mid-2002 culminated in the recording of a new four-track demo CD. Work was completed on 'Pain' and 'Thrust' by now, and the two new compositions reflected the band's current musical obsession. This time around, the trio laid down Metallica's 'Blitzkreig' and 'Lake Of Fire' by the Meat Puppets – a track that was also famously covered by Nirvana. And though the recording quality is again on the rough side, it's the sound of a band whose belief in themselves was now matched by an inter-group musical relationship becoming ever more forceful, gig on gig. Like the earlier demo, it's a thrashy offering, totally in line with the style that Matt was writing at the time. "We do have exactly ten thrash metal songs that haven't been played in years," he said subsequently. "Later we switched the style just quite naturally; it was something that just happened. It wasn't on purpose or anything, just our music grew."[20]

Things were hotting up for the band – now tearing up the clubs of the area with a full set of original tracks, give or take the odd cover version – and there was a growing realisation that Trivium was more than a mere distraction from schoolwork. "We started out as a garage band; nothing too serious," Matt explained, "but with much time and practicing we realized this is what we needed to do for life – we became serious and wrote originals, developing and practicing all the time." [21]

The work ethic has always been imperative to the band, as Travis Smith told *Rhythm Magazine*. "There's no secret to becoming a great player," he explained, "It's time and it's practice. It's not like there's a switch you can flick to get your body to do what you want."[22]

Suitably humble in approach, but with confidence soaring thanks to the band's collective approach in hitting the rehearsals with a focussed determination to develop, it was time to think about getting into a proper studio with a view to recording a high-quality demo. Something that would, hopefully, grab some media and record company interest. To that end, several gigs and rehearsals were recorded in order that the band refined the increasingly intricate nature of their original material.

In the immediacy of the live arena, it's easy enough to pull an up-for-it crowd along with you through volume and visceral performance – but a record, a 'proper release', is an entirely different matter. It has to present the music – and the band – in the best possible light and concurrently stand up to repeated playing in all manner of different contexts. People listen to music whilst doing the washing up, writing essays about Shakespeare, gettin' down 'n' dirty over the kitchen table, or driving coughy-ol' tin bucket-cars back from marching band rehearsals. Not only does the vibe have to capture the excitement of the live experience, the performances need to be flawless, the arrangement definitive and the sonic balance perfect in order to bring in another more complex layer of listener satisfaction. It's a cultural artefact and a statement of intent, a time capsule as much as it is a roaring blast of lock-n-load power. Whilst up to this point, the demos had been exactly that – demonstrations of the group's essentially live energy – the songs themselves were becoming too monstrous, too far-reaching, and too ambitious to be tamed without the added hand of a specialist collaborator. It was time for Trivium to put themselves under the tutelage of a producer whose knowledge of the technical wizardry of the recording studio and the metal genre would help the band realise the increasing quality and complexity of the tracks Matt Heafy was beginning to write.

It was long-term drinking buddy Ritchie Brown who was to come up with a suggestion for such a character, thus starting a mutually beneficial producer-band relationship that's continued throughout Trivium's explosive recording career.

That man is Jason Suecof, and he is one of the fundamental keys to Trivium's success.

"He was one of my friends," explains Brown, "he'd moved to Orlando from Connecticut. When they asked me where to record, as far as metal goes, at the time I didn't know anyone better than Jason Suecof. His speciality is metal, but I know he doesn't want anybody to think that because he wants to record a lot of other music. But it seems to be that he's doomed to record metal forever!"

Suecof – an accomplished guitarist himself – was operating from Audiohammer studios in Sanford (population: almost definitely more than seven, probably quite a lot more than that), which on first approach doesn't look the most hi-tech of set-ups. "His studio's a real shack at the back of his house," says George Moore. "It looks really shitty on the outside but when you walk in it's like: BAM! A nice big room with a hardwood floor for drum tracking and things like that, and there's a cool vocal room. It is a really comfortable environment to be recording in, as far as studios go."

Jason Suecof may be an exceptional engineer and knob twiddler, but he also possesses something that's crucial in his job: the ability to mesh in with the band dynamic, to keep the sessions running with flair and confidence whilst making it a fun experience for all concerned. And that, more than anything else, is what is at the heart of the production process. His own take on how he met the band is typical of the sense of humour that both relaxed the young group and kept things rolling on nicely. "I met them in a gay bar," the wheelchair-bound producer teased. "Matt said 'Dude, you're hot and crippled and sexy... fuckin' touch it!' No, Ritchie referred me to Trivium. By then I'd done a couple of things, I knew the metal sound and that they'd been to a couple of studios, but they hadn't got the sound they wanted." [23]

"He's really funny in a kinda juvenile, toilet humour sort of way."

George Moore elaborates on the professionalism and, uh, highbrow humour Suecof brings to the job. "Jason's like any producer," muses Moore, "he just gets the shit done. If you're doing something wrong he's not afraid to be a dick about it. He's really funny in a kinda juvenile, toilet humour sort of way. I noticed he does say 'balls' a lot. He will add 'balls' as a suffix to anything." Alex Vieira agrees. "I think *unique* is a good way to describe him. His sense of humour and the way he carries himself, you know, he's a very funny guy – very outspoken – he's not gonna beat around the bush for any reason. When he's talking to you, he's gonna tell you straight what he thinks about you. He's all over the place, too, a bit crazy – but in a good way. He is a very vocal person; he's always voicing his mind, his opinion. He's an extremely talented and creative guy."

That talent is eulogised upon by music lawyer and manager Justin Arcangel (of whom more later), whose Dark Angel Management were later to sign the producer. "Jason not only brings a passion for producing, recording, engineering, arranging, writing and playing music into each and every project, he also brings a committed and professional work ethic," their myspace site cites. "He began studying and playing guitar at eight years old and can identify with musicians in the studio that are looking to make their projects meaningful and special. Jason's

35

natural musical talent and ability, combined with his technical professional experience and work ethic, gives him the truly unique ability to work with up and coming artists as well as the more seasoned veteran artists"[24]

Musicianship, jokes about balls and a huge lump of talent from all concerned in the process would appear to constitute a perfect combination for a recording session. It was a blend of elements that boded exceptionally well for what would be a demo that was to change the lives of all associated with Trivium.

3

Demo Brio

The sessions began in earnest at Audiohammer on December 17, 2002, with Brent, Travis and Matt bursting at the seams at the prospect of taking the sound to a higher level. The seven tracks that comprised the band's most professional efforts to date show both a progression from the early howling aggression and a light touch of arrangement that speaks volumes of the band's collective musical intelligence. With Suecof at the helm, the performances are astonishingly expressive, full of a shimmering, confrontational verve and brio that are light years ahead of their self-recorded or low-budget demos of the previous years. In one form or another, these riffs had been debuted in live appearances for the previous eight months, and the time spent analysing recordings of such performances had been well-spent. But then, Matt always was a good student. These were as close to the 'definitive' Trivium sound as anything up to that point; and it was an ecstatic bunch of musicians that took the final mixes away from Suecof's ramshackle studio to gleeful stereos over the holiday period.

Although studio time was evidently at a premium in order to keep costs down, there's nary a sense of the material being rushed. Pre-production chats between Heafy, the band and Suecof had led to an understanding of the direction the songs needed to take well before the recording sessions commenced in earnest, and though there's an element of crafted improvisation to some of the solo work, the sheer power that opens the demo brings a touch of the ominous to the first track, 'To Burn The Eye'. Indeed, there's a new sense of melodicism (sic) throughout the seven minute behemoth that offsets the utter heftiness of the prog-tinged blood-sludge that forms the song. "I don't know where that came from. It could be from listening to bands like Fuel and Virgos Merlot when I first got into music," Heafy said, "that could be where I got the melody from."[25]

The energy is ramped up to the maximum through 'Requiem', softer verse structures smashing into double-pedalled, harmonic breakdowns, heart-bumping choruses and the singer showing that his vocal chords are finally beginning to catch up to the menace of delivery that he'd been yearning to achieve over the preceding two years since Travis had insisted on making him lead vocalist.

The drummer's prescience is even more justified through old favourite 'Fugue', as Heafy utilises both his tyrannosaurus scream and a spot-on pitched 'n' sung vocal to create an atmospheric workout which reflects the song title. Not only is it catchy as hell, but the bassline is a stormer, and if ever there were a blueprint for the scrunching union between the dirty and the relatively clean vocal style that Heafy was developing so well, it's captured to its fullest here. Exploring themes of aggression and self-examination on the pure-metal of 'My Hatred' gives something of an insight into the thought processes of the songwriter; there's merely a single verse but the taut and terse delivery by the vocalist allows the band to hammer through it with a lithe muscularity that has not an ounce of unnecessary fat to it.

The astonishing leap that the band had taken is showcased perfectly by the awesome acoustic-to-electric mega-riffed and barely-controlled metal chaos of 'The Storm', backed mightily by the solo-heavy 'Sworn', with Heafy's guitar work free and flying under the multi-tracking possibilities of Audiohammer, playing to his utmost through a Peavey Triple X amp on the suggestion of his producer. And boy, does he reach for the stars here. This is a group whose output is beginning to approach their vision, and a trio whose technical skill is starting to scrape at the beckoning and fiery skies of the future. It only remains for Heafy to growl his way through the inventive hell-bound 'Demon', and it is done.

With elements of In Flames as much in evidence as the influence of the classic metallers the band hold so dear, and Testament-type yowling gnarliness clawing at the sides of Killswitch Engage, it's a demo that stands as unique in the convergence of its influences into a package that holds both freshness and familiarity. Thrash, metalcore and Gothenburg-style melodic structures: three paths – all as important and all as potent as each other. The band were living up to their name in the most impressive of ways, and putting down a marker as to what they were really all about.

As soon as Janus turned his head to the new dawn of 2003, Trivium took the final mixes to Tampa, where on

January 2, the disc was mastered at Morrisound studios – putting the Altamonte Springs boys on the same level as acts like Iced Earth, who had worked there previously (and with whom the band's path would soon cross).

The mastering process brings an added sheen to proceedings; in a sense, another layer of EQ is added in order to ensure that the volume is more consistent, to fully expand the power of the final mixes when played back on differing quality home audio systems. In Trivium's case, the inherent force of the intricate dynamics of the songs was boosted a hundred fold by a professional mastering job. It all further reinforces the strong case that the 2003 'Demo' is worthy of consideration as an album – or at the very least an extended EP – in its own right.

"Oh Matt, what are you doing man, come on!"

A demo of this quality, of course, also needs comparable artwork, as well as the perfect artist to complement the blast and brilliance of the music itself. The band scouted around for possible people who'd be both consistent with their own superbly professional musical output, as well as understand the underlying ideas behind the band and their dreams. With the need to bring together all the promotional elements to back the release of the demo coherently also came the need for a redesign of their own website. Luckily, there was a guy who fitted the bill on both counts, the Swedish artist and designer Fredrik Kreem.

Kreem had been running the influential website www.swedishmetal.net since 1995, and was widely considered a major force in the dissemination of information about the Scandinavian scene. He'd also recently completed work on the site of one of Matt Heafy's favourite acts of the time, as Travis recalled. "We were looking for a website designer – Matt is a huge fan of In Flames – and Fredrik did In Flames' website. We ended up hooking up with him trying to get a website done, sent him some music of ours, that's kinda how we met."[26]

Kreem's design for the demo CD features an intriguing photograph of Trivium, capturing a real moment in time: the group are fresh-faced and just a little wide-eyed. Friend and geetar-duelling partner George Moore laughs paternally at the snapshot: "There's such a funny picture of them playing, on the back of it – you'd never know it was the same band, cause they were all about the metal back then."

"I was actually catching Matt when he was starting to get into the nu-metalcore thing that was rising. He was listening to all these bands like As I Lay Dying and Every Time I Die, and he was like 'These bands are great, and I've just been listening to Pantera and Metallica and In Flames my whole life.' And I did the exact opposite – from listening to hardcore shit to getting into old metal! I caught him during that phase, he was cutting his hair and like stretching out his ears and shit. I was like, 'Oh Matt, what are you doing man, come on!'"

Artwork duly sorted, the demo began to gather some interest from webzines and local press, with reviews and interviews starting to trickle in. "It's hard not to be cynical when reviewing demos, cause let's face it, most bands suck," said a reviewer at www.metaljudgement.com, aptly rating it as four skulls out of five, "but Trivium clearly have some talent aboard; they have the qualities to satisfy both the avid metalcore junkie and the fanatical leather jacket-wielding metal-head."[27]

A reviewer named Reno of the Heavy Metal Appreciation Society's website – www.hmas.org – took it a step further, eulogising that "these guys bring a tear to my eye. Being an American, I am, understandably, ashamed of the vast majority of what is passed off as 'metal' in this country. Trivium is a band that totally destroys that misconception. If this is only a taste of what these young metallers have to offer, then my mouth is watering."

"Not yet February, and I already have a contender for best album submission of the year," Reno continued. "Trivium have a long future ahead of them, and I personally can't wait to see how they do."[28] On the www.swedishmetal.com site, the reaction was also more than favourable, with writer Mikael upbeat about the release, albeit going a little crazy with the exclamation marks: "Wow, there is still hope for the future of the metalscene! (sic) Here is a new band from Florida with the right attitude and songwriting skills to go all the way!"[29]

Necrometal webzine was similarly enamoured by the release, writing that "the production and look of this demo is something worth paying for," and regarding one of Brian Heafy's promo extras also included in the package, "you get a pen that's cool too," continued the reviewer – who rated the demo as a muscular nine out of ten.

With such positive reactions from the metal webzines, Trivium continued to conquer the live arena; but with the demo sounding so complete, so full on and with plenty of intricate guitar work, the three-piece band were once more looking for that elusive second guitarist to bolster the sound. In February, 2003, they backed Orlando heavyweights 5 Billion Dead at the Hard Rock Live venue. Alex Vieira, guitarist with that band, remembers it well.

"I'm backstage, getting my things together, we're hanging out, waiting for our time to play. And then they approached me and asked me to join. Not a lot of people know that. They felt the need for another guitar player;

it would make their sound bigger, heavier and much better. So before we played, Travis and Matt asked me to join their band and said, 'We like the way you play...' I was quite honoured. It was like, 'Ow, that's really nice of you guys to ask me that'. It was a bit crazy that it was backstage at the Hard Rock Live in Orlando!"

It wasn't the right time for the Brazilian-born Vieira, however, with his main act generally considered the major players in the area at that time. "I was really committed to 5 Billion Dead," he continues. "I didn't give them a straight 'yes or no' answer right away. I asked them for a few days to think about it. It wasn't really a big deal to me, because I was really committed to my band at the time. I was really good friends with them but I didn't think it was the right thing for me to do."

Whilst Trivium were – like so many young bands – trying to complete their line-up with the best possible players, their web designer Fredrik Kreem – despite being three thousand miles away – was busy working on T-shirt and Poster artwork for them.

"I think the internet is what makes a lot of bands have a chance."

Technology has always been important to the band, as Matt explained. "The website is the very thing that gets Trivium to other countries faster than any other media," he told *Blistering*, an online metal 'zine, "I think for the fact that people anywhere can listen to our songs, see what we look like, read about us, and talk to us in a matter of milliseconds is astounding. I think the internet is what makes a lot of bands have a chance."[30]

Not content with merely designing the band's visuals, Kreem was also busy elsewhere. "As many of you know,

I have been very busy working with the young American Metal group Trivium," he posted on his website on May 8, 2003, "MKH Productions, Inc – Trivium's management and production company – and I have spent countless hours on web site design, development, promotions and we launched the Trivium site this past January." "Utilizing my contacts across the world, Kreem Design and Swedish Metal were key forces behind the announcement and worldwide press release today of Trivium signing a deal with the German label, Lifeforce Records. My association with MKH Productions and Trivium has been excellent and I am sure we will do much more business together in the future. I am very happy to have helped Trivium to get signed and will be looking forward to hearing great things to come from them. They are a young talented group of metal musicians and I have enjoyed helping out where I can."[31]

Stefan Luedicke, onto whom Kreem had passed Trivium's demo, is the founder and owner of German metal label Lifeforce Records. He is also a fundamental key to the band's success.

"I decided in pretty much a second that I wanted to work with this band."

"Fredrik pushed me to check these guys out," Luedicke recalled exclusively for this book, "and the first time I heard their self-released demo CD I was totally blown away from the quality that material already had. I heard how old the guys were at the time also: I couldn't believe it, and I decided in pretty much a second that I wanted to work with this band."

"What I am mainly looking for is originality, I am always looking for something new that could also work on a bigger scale," he continues. "The second important thing a band should have is the will to work hard and tour a lot. What sense does it make to have an amazing band nobody will ever know about? Because nobody will ever seen them live."

And so it came to pass that in May 2003 – mere months after recording and releasing their first high-quality demo – Trivium had snagged a record deal. This, indeed, is where things start to pick up at an astonishingly fast pace for the band. This is a pivotal point, where the Trivium project can be considered to have begun to mesh in with the dreams of stardom and mega-status that had fuelled the group during the struggles of the previous years. However, the act's young songwriter still had academic commitments to fulfil.

"I was doing really, really good in school, and Trivium was just a side thing," Matt Heafy told *Orlando Weekly*, "but once Trivium got serious, all my time went to Trivium. My grades started to go a bit, but I still stuck them up pretty high. School's always been kind of easy for me."[32]

Travis Smith, meanwhile, having graduated from Lake Brantley High a couple of years previously, was scratching his days away working in a retirement home as a waiter, as well as indulging in a bit of landscaping and carpentry on the side. Whilst the band had signed that often-elusive record deal, day-to-day life hadn't changed a great deal for the musicians themselves. Not that he wasn't averse to enjoying himself whilst he earned his corn, as he told *Metal Update*.

"I think the best job I ever had was being a secretary for a lawyer," laughed the sticksman, "that job was fucking great. I was dating her daughter and we actually worked together, so there would be many days when my boss would be like, 'Oh, take my daughter shopping' and I would get paid for that. Or, 'Take my daughter to the beach, you guys go have fun,' you know? Not really having to work, but she'd still pay us. That was fucking awesome. I had that all the way through high school – that was pretty cool… I lucked out on that one there."[33]

A sentiment with which many agree. Jammy little sod. However, with sessions for the album mooted for June 2003, the band continued the search for a guitar partner for Matt. And it was an old friend to which they turned. George Moore, he of the Hardcore vs Metal duel with Matt Heafy, had been living in his hometown of Daytona during Trivium's ascent, concentrating on his main band – the acclaimed act The Autumn Offering. But he was still in contact with 'Metal Matt'.

"I still talked to Matt Heafy online," says Moore, "he sent me an IMs [instant message] me one day and says, 'Hey George, how would you like to audition to be our second guitar player for Trivium?' – this is when they were signed to Lifeforce already. And I said, 'Oh yeah, that might be cool, sure. I got nothing else to do, and Autumn Offering's not really doing much, and you're in Orlando – not too far away.' So I went over there and ran through some stuff with them, he taught me 'Fugue', and he was like, 'Alright! You're in!' Trivium was like a fluke [for me], they asked if I wanted to join and I was kinda like, 'Yeah, why not. You guys are cool, I'll try that.'"

Problem solved, then. Trivium had become a Quadivium. And there was the small matter of a debut album to record.

4

sparks start
to fly

To all intents and purposes, however, it was the three-piece Trivium that had inked the deal with Lifeforce, the trio that had written, rehearsed, tweaked and perfected the songs, and therefore Brent, Matt and Travis were the band that set down the tracks that would become their debut album, Ember To Inferno. With Suecof's skill behind the desk, the growing relationship between the producer and his young charges was set to have explosive results.

Heafy's approach to songwriting had an inherent maturity and panache, which is evident throughout an album that explores often dark psychological themes. But writing was second nature to the guitar shredder, as he explained to *Pitriff*. "Musically, it's always like, I'll just sit

51

down, write a riff, and then – it's cool, because the whole song's played out in my head. It's a really easy process to write, it's not like it's half-assed or anything, it's just a fluid and natural process, writing a song to me, and that's what always comes out."

"From there, I'll usually play with the music and listen to what I hear melodically, and I'll come up with a melody and fit words for it that always have something I'll feel very passionately about. A lot of the things on *Ember…* are about people breaking free from the standards and going after the dreams they want: very positive and motivational for us, those songs on *Ember…*"[34]

Four tracks had survived from the 'Demo' release – 'To Burn The Eye', 'My Hatred', 'Requiem' and 'Fugue' were all re-recorded in a more refined form, the latter opus once more re-titled, this time as 'Fugue (A Revelation)'. Bolstered by seven new songs, it's an LP that again shows a masterful progression from what had come before. Suecof's musical skills are even more evident on this album, playing keyboards on 'Inception, The Bleeding Skies" and 'A View Of Burning Empires'. 'Inception,' a twenty second, gothy introduction resonant with a tense expectation, was conceived fairly late in proceedings.

"The title track 'Ember To Inferno' is about the development of Trivium in our eyes."

"Jason Suecof broke out the keyboard and started doing the background parts. So that part came out really easy, and I kind of fought for the intro part, but nobody else wanted an intro – they just wanted to start with 'Pillars Of Serpents,'" Matt explained, "so what we did, we took the outro, reversed it, and then there's 'Inception, The Bleeding Skies'.' And what I did was listen to both of them

52

and just wrote some words that I thought were suitable for the parts, just some soft scenery that I listened to."[35]

'Pillar Of Serpents' is as close to a statement of intent as you are likely to find for the first 'proper' track on a debut album. As riff after riff is thrown into the mix, elements of metalcore growl, that Scandi-metal vibe and a tense stand-off between melodic choruses and multi-layered guitar work rush it on at a kickin' pace. At times it's Maiden; at times Metallica; at times Arch Enemy; at times Smith's pacy double-kick drumming smashes the track firmly into the thrash metal arena. It's everything that Trivium was about, and everything that they were to become. Similarly, 'If I Could Collapse The Masses' is fiery, frantic, mighty and melodic. The solo herein is pure Dave Murray, and Travis' stamina in the busy, bustling, blasting drum part is wickedly wonderful. The complex 'Fugue' and utterly catchy, classic metal-isms of 'Requiem' are as full of spiky aggression and crackling power as they had ever sounded. By the time the band tackle the sombre magnificence of the title track, complete with tremolo picking and harmonic solos (one courtesy of Suecof himself) it's clear that this is an act of some quality, rendered all the more incredible given that they were all just about still in their teens.

"The title track 'Ember To Inferno' is about the development of Trivium in our eyes," explained Heafy, "I know it isn't the biggest thing to others, but the song is about how Trivium started as such a small thing in our lives – but now it's become more than just a hobby; it's all we think about and work for in life. The song came before the album title, and we just felt that it was a good title."[36] "It has been named as an anthem track: *THE* Trivium song. I think that's because this song [quickly] shows everything we're capable of. It's like a sampler of the things we can throw into a song – and still keep maximum organization: speed, heaviness, solos, harmonies, clean vocals, catchiness, screaming... it's got a little bit of everything. It's a very straightforward song."[37]

After a short interlude with the guitar instrumental, 'Ashes', we're ready for part 2 of the LP. In the days of records, this would be the end of side A (fact: for those born after 1990, 'records' are like a big, easily-broken version of a CD, except with music on both sides. They are usually made of a black substance called 'vinyl', whose best friends are dust, lint and things that scratch the surface. You will need to buy something called a 'record player' in order to listen to these strange beasts).[38]

The grandiose themes, ultra-confrontational dissonance between light and dark musicality through these guitar-driven, sky-shattering songs hammers 'To Burn The Eye' into the listener's head with a forceful determination to excite.

Travis's double bass work ramps up 'Falling To Grey', which features one of Matt's favourite solos. "It's very fluid and legato," he explained to *Guitar World*, "and it gives off a sense of reluctance in between the runs. It almost has its own shy emotion in between bursts of fast shredding."[39] 'My Hatred' retains all of its thrashy power, and the album is nearly complete.

'When All Light Dies' features a brilliant solo, in line with much of *Ember To Inferno*. Trivium's love for the shred marked them out as rather unique at the time. "I think guitar solos are 'cool' and that more people should take the time to do them, be original and express your own voice through your instrument," Heafy told *Unbound Zine*. "Solos in our music are pretty essential. But we don't have solos just to have them; all the solos on *Ember* and the 'Demo' CD were carefully thought out and express melody and emotion (even the fast shreddy ones). I'm noticing more bands here and there throwing solos in, but you can tell there isn't much time they took to consider melody and emotion – it was just there to do it."[40]

Interestingly, the solo here is provided by Alex Vieira, who Matt had approached to join Trivium earlier that year. "I knew they were in the studio but I wasn't really close to the band to the point where I could just go and hang out with the guys and see the recording process," he explains. "It was one of those things where they called me and said 'Hey, are you available Tuesday?' or whatever day it was, cause they were gonna be in the studio all day."

"They asked me, 'Hey, do you wanna come down and track a solo for us? We have a song that's done, pretty much,'" says Vieira. "Matt told me, 'I don't have anything written for it, as far as the lead goes.' I didn't even know the song! I just got there, they played me the track a few times and Matt showed me the part where the solo was going to be. Two or three takes went by, off the cuff. I looked at Matt, and I was like, 'Dude, if you like it, it's a keeper. Just let it roll.' I was playing, and then looking at them to see the reaction – to see if they liked what I was doing. After all, it's their album and I wanted the guys to be happy."

"They asked me, 'Hey, do you wanna come down and track a solo for us?'"

"A lot of times in situations like this I tend to improvise," he continues, "then go back and listen to what I did, pick the parts I like and then do another coupla takes. Make that original idea better, or take that original idea and make something bigger, you know? It ended up working out that way. Since I didn't know the song, I had no previous ideas or preconceptions on what the solo was going to sound like, because I had no idea which direction the song was taking, you know, the vibe of the song. It turned out the way it did and everyone was happy. I was very happy with it."

The quality of the solo is undeniable: Vieira is a master of his craft, and would – in another universe – have been a massive asset to Trivium had he decided to join them as second guitarist. The glimpse of talent shown here meshes perfectly with the track, the album and the band's developing sound. At this point he, on paper, could still have become a member as he still hadn't actually told Trivium he wasn't interested in joining the group long-term!

"Don't let George do anything on the album cause he's not officially in the band yet, blah blah blah!"

"It's something that was never discussed openly between the band and I," he recalls wistfully. "It was kinda one of those things where I asked for some time to think about it, and I never really got back to them. So technically I didn't really say no! It was odd. I didn't feel like I wanted to hurt anyone's feelings by saying, 'No thanks, I don't wanna do this,' and at the same time I thought it would be better for them to find someone else. Someone younger or someone who was more into the kind of music they were doing at the time – which was a little bit different."

"It was strange, cause I was so committed to the music I was doing at the time in my own band [5 Billion Dead], I didn't wanna give up on that and move on to another project that was already started by someone else in a completely different style. But I neglected the fact that the band wanted a yes or no – I never gave them an answer. That's something I need to talk to Matt about!

I need to apologise cause I never gave him an answer and I felt bad afterwards."

Ember To Inferno comes to an end with the acoustic comedown of 'A View Of Burning Empires', which brings matters to a laid-back, nostalgic head. It also features George Moore, who – in contrast to Alex Vieira – had subsequently agreed to join Trivium when they asked him to fill that troublesome rhythm guitar slot.

"Originally I wasn't supposed to do a single thing on the album," laughs Moore, "I was just kinda hanging out in the studio; it was like direct orders from Heafy's dad: 'Don't let George do anything on the album cause he's not officially in the band yet, blah blah blah!' And I was fine with that."

"But they were trying to do this rhythm acoustic guitar part. There was a lot of barreing and you had to change positions a coupla times. The only thing I can think of is that Heafy and Suecof tried to do it before me... it was sounding a little mucky, and neither of them were satisfied with how it was going."[41]

"Heafy and Suecof totally outshred me on guitar – they're amazing, and I would love to be able to play like them – I was like, 'Hey let me try' and I pulled it off! Cause most of the time, at home, I don't sit and run through lots of sweeps and scales and arpeggios and do a lot of the shredding thing, I actually sit down with my acoustic guitar and play barre chords. I guess my hand was just feeling stronger than theirs that day. I sat down and did it in like three takes. Then Jason listened to it and was like, 'Alright, you're on the album now.' It was kind of a fluke, it wasn't supposed to happen, but they just needed the part to sound right and they were in a hurry. I was the only one around who could do it."

Matt later described the *Ember...* experience as "two weeks of fun with some disaster. My guitar wouldn't stay in tune, equipment was breaking, etcetera. Aside from that it was fun – it's great to hear songs you hear in the rehearsal space all of the sudden sound huge."[42]

With recording complete – and mastering sessions taking place at Morrisound Studios between July 1 and 16 (Matt having to rest up awhile after giving the vocals his absolute all, was consequently unable to communicate in anything above a whisper) – it was time to get back out and hit it live as a four-piece.

"I learned the whole album, or most of the album – enough to play a set with them cause they needed me for a show," remembers George Moore. "I did that for about a month or two, and I was still going back to Daytona. Now I think of it, it was quite stressful with all the driving, cause I was still trying to play with The Autumn Offering, and record a new demo with them and stuff."

Subsequently Matt announced to the world, through Lifeforce Records' website, that "it is no longer a secret. For those of you who saw our set Saturday, August 2nd – yes – we added a rhythm guitarist – that is George, George Moore our newest addition! George has joined the Trivium team as its rhythm guitarist and back-up vocalist. George, 19 years old, comes to us by way of The Autumn Offering (who by the way is a major kick ass hardcore band)."[43]

It was to be a short-lived show of strength: Moore's tenure as second guitarist turned out to be rather shorter than anybody could have predicted. "I played a show with Trivium, and it went over pretty good, and it was fun," he explains, "but I had a show booked with The Autumn Offering a few days later with Hatebreed in Tampa. This was the fourth time they'd let us open up for them."

"We'd finished our new demo by then, and we gave it to Jamie Jasta. He listened to it on his bus, and came out and said 'You guys are signed to Stillborn now!' And I was like, 'Holy Shit, I'm in two signed bands now. That's not gonna be good!'"

"So I immediately called Matt Heafy and said, 'Hey, just so you know, Jamie's just kinda signed The Autumn Offering to Stillborn.' And he was like, 'Really? Oh FUCK! Let me talk to my dad and call you back.'"

"Then Heafy calls me the next day and he's like, 'Yeah, uh, it's probably better for both bands if you just stay with The Autumn Offering since you've been doing that for longer, and that's your thing.' Which I agreed with, cause it *was* my thing, I was writing the songs and I would rather stay with something that I'd been doing for a long time rather than just like hop on someone else's band like I was pretty much doing with Trivium. So I did that, and they let me go and I was totally cool with it."

"Really? Oh FUCK! Let me talk to my dad and call you back."

With Vieira and Moore both out of the picture, the problematic post of second guitarist was once again up for grabs. But this time, the band chose well.

Corey Beaulieu was born on November 22, 1983 in Brunswick, Maine (population: definitely split roughly between males and females, some of whom probably also own pets. And cars. And houses and stuff. Some might even have a Trivium promo pen.) He'd been playing guitar since he was fourteen, studying on his own as well as taking two and a half years of lessons to bolster his technique. Beaulieu's initial brush with loud music was also something of an eye-opener.

Raising himself on a diet of Guns N' Roses, Metallica and Megadeth, the hard rock and metal fan found that his growing talent on the guitar opened up more musical possibilities. Every step of the way, his love for the heavyweights of the genre inspired him to practice harder and refine his skills to the highest strata possible.

He was already becoming an accomplished guitarist when he moved to Florida in 2002. Newly graduated from high school, he set about finding some local gigs that would make his head fizz. In one of those happy coincidences that often permeate life and success, one of the first concerts he caught featured Trivium. Liking what he heard, Corey soon began following the band at their local shows. With a common musical grounding, Beaulieu and the band were bound to get chatting in the bars of Lost & Found and the like, and soon became good mates. So when the band were looking for a new member, a lightbulb appeared over Corey's head. Ping!

"The only thing that I wanted to do was be in a band."

"They finished the record when they were looking for a second guitar player to join the band," Beaulieu told *Metal Force*, "because at that time they were a three-piece. A lot of stuff like harmonies and guitar stuff live just didn't have the same power as the recording. So they wanted to add another guitar player. I knew Matt and I'd seen the band play for a year before I joined. I knew Matt a bit as we talked on and off and when I saw they were looking for a guitar player, I just called them up, jammed and it all worked out from there."

For a change, the Trivium family had found a willing guitarist who could commit full-time to the group. "Being into guitar and heavy metal music, the only thing that I wanted to do was be in a band," Beaulieu continued. "Back in high school I had some bands but nothing serious or anything. Just garage bands and high school stuff. This is my first real band." [44]

Covering all bases, he spoke to his immediate predecessor, George Moore, about how best to make the union happen. "I'd talk to him online every now and again," chuckles Moore, "before he joined them he was asking me questions about what he should do and how he should act. Which is really funny cause he outshreds me horribly! Corey's a way better guitar player than I am."

The addition of Beaulieu found favour with their record company, too, as Stefan Luedicke explains. "At the time we signed Trvium it was a three-piece band only," he says, "and as *Ember To Inferno* came out Corey joined the band, which was a big step forward. Not that the band wasn't great before already!"

Corey's debut gig as a member of Trivium was at a sold-out show at Hard Rock Live, Orlando on September 5, 2003. That date was auspicious for another reason: the group unveiled a brand new track, 'Like Light To The Flies'. Heafy enjoyed the experience immensely as "there were about 2000 people there – people went absolutely insane when we played. Everything was perfect." [45]

At this stage, Trivium's activities were confined to rehearsing, playing and partying round Florida. But that was soon to change, with Lifeforce bringing the band over to Europe for a mini-tour during October. Not only was it the band's first time playing outside the United States, it was also their first time outside their home state. Some jump to make!

"The first time I had a feeling of how great this band could be in its future was as they came over for a short Euro trip," offers Luedicke, "even if it was the first time for them playing outside of Florida, it was simply amazing to see them playing live. It was like they never did anything else before, and even though it was on a very DIY level, they filled the room with so much energy it was just a pleasure to see them playing."

"The best show for us was in Saalfeld, Germany on our European mini-tour," agreed Heafy, "people were singing along, ninja moshing, stage diving – that was quite a sight."[46]

"This is like a taster before we get to something bigger."

During the Euro jaunt – which took in three dates in Germany, Belgium and The Netherlands – the band had also picked up a new way to describe their sound – Melodic Death Metalcore. It was a title Heafy admitted that they'd nicked "from Dew Scented. I was on their website and it had Trivium on it, and the link said 'Melodic Death Metalcore' and we liked it." [47]

In an interview that speaks volumes for the band's humility, Brent Young told the Dutch webzine *Lords Of Metal* that "it's just like getting our feet wet as far as touring and playing and doing multiple shows in a row because we haven't done that before. We normally just play on the weekends. This is like a taster before we get to something bigger."

"It's hard," admitted Matt, "man, I got nauseous on the plane, nauseous on the ride here, nosebleeds, six hour time-difference – but now we're here. And oh yeah, we like it."[48]

Ember To Inferno was released on October 14, 2003, and Lifeforce were very pleased with the results. "My opinion is that the fact all the members were that young by the time *Ember To Inferno* was recorded made it what it is," says Luedicke. "You can hear the band is fresh and pretty much like a rough diamond – they were still trying out a lot of things. You even hear the influences of all these classic metal acts and almost no influences from current always similar-sounding metal(core) acts, because Matt was simply not listening to stuff like that by the time the record was made. I think that makes *Ember To Inferno* different from other releases that came out around the same time."

The press feedback to the album started rolling in, to the delight of the singer. "We've had so many reviews and we have read them all [over 80 already]," he told *Metal Reviews*, "a majority of the reviews have been pretty positive and supportive. From country to country (as far as Romania to Japan; Belgium to Spain; Mexico to Canada) people are loving the album, we get a steady stream of emails from people who want to buy it and the demo CD and just to say they liked what they heard."

"I think what's really exciting for people is the promise of a good future and since we had a pretty strong debut, I hope to live up to everyone's standards (which I'm sure are high). We've been gaining comparisons to some of our favourites like In Flames, Arch Enemy, Megadeth, Metallica, Shadows Fall etc, and it's just the biggest compliment."[49]

Stereokiller's review of the album couldn't have been more gushing. "I cannot believe this wonderful, wonderful music is created by three people," wrote the breathless journalist. "This CD is an absolute masterpiece. Mixing classical metal stylings with New England style metal, Swedish melodic death metal, and even a bit of power metal, this shit had my jaw on the floor the entire time. They may pay tribute to their influences, but they run wild with the imagination and took my breath away, as I'm sure they will yours as well."[50] Long-time supporters www.hmas.org were similarly impressed, giving the LP full marks with the strapline that "every song on this album is gold. There is not one single second of filler, here. These guys have an extraordinary amount of talent."[51]

"This CD is a powerhouse from track one through track twelve," offered *Rough Edge*, "delivering a solid melodic death metal/metalcore performance that never lightens up and, thankfully, never goes too far extreme. Guitars thunk along at a jackhammer pace, drums thump with a deadly rhythm and – son of a bitch! – you can understand most of the lyrics! Hell, there are even some catchy melodic choruses here."[52]

"You get the complete package, which constitutes a killer CD, worth each cent," wrote a German journalist, "great presentation, killer solos, breathtaking compositions with unbelievable precision, hooks, riffs and rhythms and a 'take no prisoners' attitude."[53] *Unrestrained* 'zine summed it all up neatly: "the sound is flawless in its approach, it's original as hell, and it's damn near perfect."[54]

The group's Euro jaunt had been a lot of fun, but gig-wise Trivium weren't as active as they'd like. Undaunted, they kept up with the rehearsals and the songwriting, and were ready to rock once more, and the year drew to a close with some extra demo recording sessions during the thanksgiving holiday period – November 26 to 30 – the quartet spending time with Suecof in Audiohammer and laying down three new tracks: 'The Deceived', 'Blinding Tears Will Break The Skies' and 'Like Light To The Flies'.

All in all, 2003 had been a pretty damned big year for Trivium. But nobody could have predicted what 2004 was to bring.

5

faster miles an hour

As 2004 dawned, Brian Heafy began spreading the word about the new album in his inimitable way, postering and flyering anything that moved (and if it didn't move, postering it until it did). The positive press coverage – particularly in Europe – was keeping things ticking over sweetly.

"Brian was paying for ads in *Guitar One* magazine for them, making postcards for the new album, having them passed out at places," says George Moore. "Brian was all about the promotion really. He did a good job, and he went about it really well. He definitely put a lot of his own money into it. Of course, it's obviously paid off, cause look at him now, right? Point is, you can have all the money in the world but if you're promoting crap it's gonna get you nowhere." "It's fantastic," added Matt, "he invests so much in the band because he really cares about it. We're so lucky!"[55]

One of Brian's flyers was to find its way into the pocket of someone who is also crucial to Trivium's success. That guy is Dale Resteghini of Raging Nation films. A respected actor and video producer, his work had been shown all over the multitude of post-millennial music channels. Something of a growing legend himself, he was beginning to be a sought-after professional for both young and established bands. The New York native – in one of those moments of synchronicity that often defines success – had first randomly crossed paths with Trivium late the previous year.

"It was the fall of 2003, maybe October, November. There was a metal fest in Avebury Park, New Jersey," revealed Resteghini for this book. "I was on my way to see Precious Blood, who I was getting ready to do a video for. I was there seeing all kinds of heavy, heavy bands play. I happened to be walking around and looked down on the ground cause I stepped on a postcard, and it was for Trivium. The artwork even then looked like they were maybe a Swedish metal band, or something like that, because of how the font was and whatnot."

"You go to these things, and you see that stuff everywhere," he continues, "and for whatever reason that stuck with me, I put it in my pocket. I looked to see if they were playing that day - they weren't. So I get home, I check out the Trivium website, to hear the music and see some visuals. I just figured [they were from Europe] cause I saw Lifeforce and I knew that was a European label."

"I sent them an email introducing myself – I was just coming off doing Hatebreed – so I had a lot of juice going that Fall, even though it was early in my career. I got an email back a few days later from Brian, saying they'd heard about me and they were looking to work with me at some point. He said basically that he was looking to spend what little money they had on putting them on the road for a year, or – until I reached out to them, perhaps, maybe even do a video."

The initial excitement engendered by the signing of the Lifeforce deal and the subsequent European 'tour' to support *Ember To Inferno* was subsiding somewhat, although Matt Heafy commented that the relationship with their record label was "great," offering that, "people all around the world are hearing us – and in turn we hear good things back from them. We're still both new in our relationship and we hope that everything goes nice and big from here."[56] "It seems like every review, in general, has been unanimous. All countries seem to be very positive; we've had very positive and impressed views from: US, Romania, Germany, Holland, Japan, Belgium, etc. It really is amazing."[57]

Stefan Luedicke acknowledges the problems in taking Trivium to the level they so craved, however. "Of course we always want to sell a lot of records," he says, "and the band and Brian always pushed us (in a good way) to do more for the group. Unfortunately we don't have the same resources as [major] labels have to push a band as hard as they can, so we simply reached a point where we couldn't do more for them. It was harder to convince magazines and distributors about these young Florida guys. If you tell them you have something amazing to come that could be huge, most of the time the reaction is 'Yeah whatever, every label is saying that.'"

The deal in its early stages seemed to be rosy for all parties, but problems soon began to mount up with the LP less than present in Trivium's home country. "As far as US distribution is concerned," said Matt, "we did seem to have some problems getting the CD to stores like Best Buy and we know it is because no one knows who we are, so it takes the label more time to get the stores to put it on the shelf. Lifeforce worked a deal with Lumberjack and Navarre in the US among others and another dozen or so European distributors."

"For some reason there seem to be a great number of German/European record labels that are into this style of music. We have no problem getting the CD out worldwide."[58] They had an option to do a further CD with Lifeforce within twelve months, which seemed ideal as they had already written many new songs.[59]

Of course, releasing an album is only one part of the process. And for a label with a small budget, keeping their ambitious new charges in the public eye was becoming difficult. Expensive aspects such as tour support or video production exacerbated the universal restrictions of being an independent. "They basically put us in a studio and we recorded the album and that was pretty much it."[60]

With all this going through the minds of the Trivium camp, Brian Heafy called up Dale Resteghini and made a swift decision. "At this point in time they were only on Lifeforce, and I drew the conclusion that they weren't happy," says Resteghini.

"They didn't know anybody at [labels] at that point; Brian was looking to get to know some people at some labels. I did [know people]. So during a month or two of courtship we decided we were gonna do a video."

Perhaps due to the slightly frustrating label situation, the original choice of shooting a video for 'Ember To Inferno' was altered and it was decided that the new subject matter would be 'Like Light To The Flies', from the Thanksgiving 2003 demos. Again, the Trivium camp had showed great forward planning in choosing someone hungry, talented and equally ambitious with whom to work. Dale Anthony Resteghini had friends in high places.

"I had taken their CD Demo of 'Like Light To The Flies' and played it to Josh at Trustkill and some of the guys at Century Media, and everybody was like, 'Yeah, it's good, but it doesn't grab me'," explains the video director, "and I played it for my very, very good friend Jamie Jasta of Hatebreed. Everybody just kinda said, 'Well, they're good, but they don't stand out' – even though I'd said that they were young kids at that point in time."

"They basically put us in a studio and we recorded the album and that was pretty much it."

The video itself was an ambitious project.

"I'm somewhat inspired not so much by lyrics all the time as I am by music and harmonies and sounds itself," continues Resteghini. "I'm also very driven visually, always looking for amazing locations that can help make a video look a lot bigger than the budget itself."

"Matt wanted to go with some very special effects-oriented ideas, and getting lots of kids to be in the video, but I explained to him that if we got lots of kids a) it's costly, and b) you don't have a fanbase yet. So let's stick with a really good, killer performance, and a killer location, extravagant lighting – which we have with the lightning strikes, and let's settle on a cool narrative, a cool dark narrative. And the narrative itself became a sort of horror movie, which was fine."

"We shot for two days," continues the New York-based video dude, "one day for the performance, one for the narrative. This beautiful blonde girl and this guy, they happen to be lost, they drive up to this castle, they walk inside. And they end up wandering around these deep caverns of the castle, which are very much from any of those cool decent horror films. And we reveal that the guy she's with is actually a killer, he purposely loses her in a low level of the castle, she's lost, she's looking around in this room of horror, which has jars of skeleton pieces and all these crazy, horrific elements. And he ends up coming behind her, and he chains her up, we don't graphically see what he does to her but we just show a scalpel. We just show these things. It's really horrific, and it ties in great with the screaming and the solos, and all those moments."

"By the end of the day, I could not talk."

"The video was incredible, I mean, the standard I can compare it to is like, the Linkin Park video quality," Matt told *Pitriff*, "Raging Nations did an incredible job, and it was a lot of fun doing it. It was exhausting, I mean, two twelve-hour days of just playing to the same song, but it came out amazing."

"By the end of the day, I could not talk. But Dale really helped us find our live appearance. Because he's screaming at us, people call him 'Rage.' He screams at you! We learned a lot from him."[61]

Once the video was complete, Resteghini started showing it around friends and colleagues in record companies, and Brian Heafy began to fire it off to record labels. With a stunning, impact-heavy visual reference, the people who'd been lukewarm about the Thanksgiving demo now understood the incredible energy and potential Trivium possessed.

"Anybody who saw that video," says Dale, "were blown the fuck away. They couldn't believe that this was the same band. It made them look like platinum-selling metal stars!"

"Shortly after Brian had started sending it around, everybody from Tony at Victory to the people at Century Media, even to The Rev who manages Thursday and Shadows Fall, and Monte at Roadrunner, everybody was like, 'Who the fuck is this band, and who the fuck did the video?!'"

"That led to a bidding war between a bunch of labels, most notably Century Media and Roadrunner, the latter of whom won out. Everybody at Roadrunner who was part of that signing – and even Brian and Matt – will tell you that video, that relationship that began when I happened to step on their postcard, and *keeping it* – cause I don't [usually] keep stuff – turned into them getting signed to Roadrunner, and that story of them getting signed because of a Dale video has become legendary among bands in the scene. When I say legendary I mean legendary within the community."

"We went to a show recently, and Carl, Josh, all these guys who own these labels, were like, 'Dale, I'm kicking myself in the ass because I did not sign this band.'"[62]

"From that first talking with Brian and Matt we knew the band wanted something else than being on a label as Lifeforce," muses Stefan Luedicke, "which was cool for me, because it was something they never kept us in the dark about – and we accepted the fact they didn't want to sign for more than only one record with Lifeforce. As you can see now it wasn't the worst decision to make, seeing the fact the success of Trivium also helped Lifeforce a lot."

Having put the band in a position to sign with Roadrunner – their ultimate dream label – courtesy of that company's A&R men Monte Conner and Mike Glitter – Dale Resteghini also introduced Brian Heafy to another vital component in the Trivum wheel.

"When they came up here to do the video, Brian said 'Yo, do you know any good rock 'n' roll or metal attorneys?'" continues Dale, "and I just said, 'Well, I know this guy, Justin Arcangel.' Justin and he met for the first time when they came up for the video. They talked for another month, they formed Dark Angel Promotions, and now they're managers of not only Jason Suecof the producer, but also Sanctity and Trivium."

"Justin handles all the legal stuff, points the band in the right direction, goes out to find them the right kind of tours. Brian is the dad-manager who takes care of all their merchandise, their web needs, helps to research other things for them, and keeps them profitable, making them money. And then, of course you got the band who do what they're good at: making music and touring."

April 6, 2004 saw the official announcement of Trivium's signing to Roadrunner, the A&R men involved waxing lyrical about their new charges in a press release. "Trivium show an incredible maturity and finesse in their music considering the young age of songwriter, Matthew Heafy," said Monte Conner, also responsible for Sepultura, Slipknot, and Type O Negative. "I can only imagine where he will be in ten years. Plus, he has the drive, determination and smarts to match his musical muscle. Matthew and the rest of the band have grown up listening to all the acts I've signed over the years, so to have Trvium here, helping shape Roadrunner's future metal template, is a real thrill for me on a personal level."

Mike Glitter, the other A&R working with the band, extended his excitement: "Not only is Trivium a great metal band, they're a great band, period," he enthused. "At 18, Matt Heafy has a better developed sense of musical theory and melody than most successful musicians twice his age. These guys crackle with the same sort of vibe you felt about bands like Metallica or Megadeth in the 80s – out to prove that they're top of their game and willing to do what it takes to get there."

It was all smiles from the band themselves, with Heafy citing bands such as Slipknot, Machine Head, Coal Chamber, Soulfly, Sepultura and Fear Factory as major early influences. On a final note, his mission statement to Roadrunner was "Let's conquer the world!"[63]

"It was the stupidest show of our lives."

Travis Smith was similarly stoked at the prospect. "At first we couldn't believe it," he told *Orlando Weekly*. "It took about a week to finally settle in. If you could have seen the expression on our faces when we found out the news! It was like that kind of Christmas when you're five years old and you get that big huge toy that you want."[64]

Not that signing a piece of paper guaranteed to change your life stops you having the odd dodgy gig here and there. On the very day that the contract was signed, the group found themselves in less-than-salubrious circumstances, as Beaulieu explained to *Kerrang!*'s Catherine Yates.

"It was the stupidest show of our lives," he growled. "It was in the garage of a tattoo place we hadn't been to before. When we arrived, there was no PA, no mic stands, and the fans had to hold the mic up so Matt could sing and play. It was the biggest waste of time, ever. We were like 'We just signed to Roadrunner, what are we doing here?'"[65]

With things hotting up, and the prospect of Trivium's first 'proper' tour – Eurotourism aside – looming, backing God Forbid for sixteen dates across the States, it was time for some major life decisions for the young musicians, the youngest of whom had been juggling school and international rock success reasonably successfully to that point.

"I finished high school early and started college early," Matt told *Rock Sound*, "but then I had to leave as we were offered the God Forbid tour. My dad was like, 'you only get chances like this once in your life and you should take it'. I was like, 'I should stay in college', and he was like, 'No you shouldn't, you should go on tour.'[66] I was begging my teachers to let me stay in because I was already three quarters of the way through the semester, but they said no. I was majoring in business. But, oh well."[67]

"I remember right after they got signed when they decided that the band was what they wanted to do for the next few years – and see what happens," recalls Alex Vieira. "Brian said something along the lines that Matt had an option to either continue with his studies and go to college, or to take the band and go on the road and see what happens. He gave him that freedom. He knew that whichever Matt decided to do, he would apply himself 100%."

"Cause sometimes you get a one-time shot, and that's it. He was very supportive of Matt's decision to pursue that career. Which is a very tough career! A lot of people don't realise that, but it's a very tough life. Being on the road all the time, away from friends, family, not getting to sleep in your own bed. But it's a lot of fun."

"I'm sure when Trivium first started it was to have a good time," offers Ritchie Brown, "and have fun with your friends and create music together. In the beginning it was the same thing as a lot of bands. It's not until you realise how seriously you can take it, the business side and everything. I think it was once the decision was made that, 'Hey, this is what I wanna do for the rest of my life', then you know to start treating it like a career."

Strong family support also extended to Travis's dad, Mike, as Orlando Metal Awards maestro Matt Wagner recalled to the author. "The first tour, Travis' dad told me personally that he'd used Travis' college fund to help keep them on the road," Wagner remembers, "cause they weren't making any money when they first went out on the road. They were the opening band, and they had to travel from Florida to Seattle straight through to play the first gig of the tour, you know. It's a long drive!"

Long drive or not, the band were finally getting the opportunity to shred and shimmy and send shivers down the spines of all who were to experience them that April. New Jersey's God Forbid is not an act famed for their self-restraint by any means, and the young upstarts were about to find out what rock 'n' roll really meant.

"They're the ones who popped our touring cherry," Travis later recalled, "they were the first band we actually toured with and it was definitely rock 'n' roll. It was one of those tours where we partied... hard."[68] "They showed us the ROPES! They taught us how to be a real rock 'n' roll band!"[69]

"Two, three girls in public places with all the windows open, public bathrooms, sharing people."

Without being indelicate, Trivium's tastes of the sixteen-date tour were being refined day by day. That's refined as in birds, booze and rock 'n' roll behaviour.

Matt had always had a girlfriend through high school but when Trivium hit the road was just coming out of a string of bad relationships. "So I was like, 'You know what? Embrace me!' Sex is sex, man, it's all good!"

"Me, Corey and our guitar tech Ralph were really the bad guys in the band. Two, three girls in public places with all the windows open, public bathrooms, sharing people. Well, sharing one person – there were probably two or three of us... we don't do it to disrespect, we give the people what they want onstage and off."[70]

Travis elaborated that "on that God Forbid tour they picked a night for each of us and on that night they would get you completely fucked. That was their way of saying, 'OK, you can hang.'"[71]

There was also time to play some music, too, with Heafy getting up regularly onstage with the headliners to lend his vocal talent to their seminal track, 'Antihero'. "It was amazing," concluded the vocalist, "we're all really good friends after that experience. They're incredible live and really incredible people, too. So that was a lot of fun."[72]

Finding a moment to reflect on the year past, and the band's own stickability, the singer turned serious for a minute. "With us, we're all friends. We're like family, and we get in a lot of fights just like brothers would. It's like a family unit, kind of."[73]

The period of 2003 to 2004 was a vindication that it had all been worthwhile: the struggles in getting the songs together, finding a producer, signing two record deals within a year and recording a stunning debut video and album, debuting their live show in Europe and America, finally solving that troublesome second guitarist slot and putting Trivium in a position to finally turn the inferno to mind-melting heat.

But that was all soon to be shattered.

6

fever

Brent Young had been through almost as much as Matt and Travis since he'd joined up with the extremely young Trivium way back in 2001. Having slotted over from rhythm guitar to bass, and navigated the rocky early years of the band, he was surely entitled to enjoy the band's big break as much as anyone else. Three years of hard work were finally paying off and the golden glories of making this a valid career and lifestyle choice were firmly within reach.

Therefore it was a shock to all when, shortly after the God Forbid tour, Young left the band which he'd striven so hard to make a success.

"I can't imagine why he dropped out of the band [at that point]," muses Matt Wagner, "but you know, I guess he went on the road and it was hard. It's hard on the road, you're away from your girlfriend, away from your family, you've got no money, you haven't taken a shower for three or four days, you're barely making money as a band to get to the next gig. It's definitely a difficult thing – it's not for everybody."

"'Okay! You gotta do what you gotta do and we gotta do what we gotta do!'"

Travis was similarly bemused as he tried to fathom out Brent's decision to call it quits. "Brent, uhh… I think it got too real for him," he mused, "he didn't want to make this a career; he didn't want to be on the road all the time. He just wanted to live a normal life. That's the choice he made, so we supported him [in his decision]. We said, 'Okay! You gotta do what you gotta do and we gotta do what we gotta do!'"[74]

Losing a band member – and good friend – could have threatened the immediate future of Trivium. With recording sessions for their Roadrunner debut beginning to be booked – pre-production commencing on May 22 and 23 at Audiohammer – and the imminence of a tour throughout June backing Iced Earth, the band needed to move quickly to find a player who could mesh in, like, *yesterday*.

Mike Poggione was a well-known bassist who had lent his technically incandescent style to a number of metal and black metal acts during the first years of the new millennium. His main focus had been with Monstrosity, leading lights of the Florida death metal scene since the early 1990s. He'd also formed a relationship with none other than Jason Suecof, whose prog/tech metal project Capharnaum were slowly forming into something other

82

than the mess-around jams that Suecof – and his younger brother Jordan – had begun way back in 1995. Capharnaum's second album, *Fractured*, had been released on the Willowtip label on February 17, 2004, and featured a young growler on vocals by the name of... Matthew Heafy. Although making little more than a ripple on its release, the relationships formed during the Audiohammer recording sessions meant that Poggione sliding into the suddenly-vacant bass slot for Trivium was something of an inevitability.

"I was the first real candidate to try out for the job," recalled Poggione to the author for this book, "I think they had tried out two other people during the week that I had 'applied' for the job and they basically told me that the other two characters sucked balls compared to me. I jammed with them and got tabs and the music set list. I was hired to do that tour. Trivium's set allowed me to have a great time adding different aspects of my style and playing abilities."

The Iced Earth tour further served to bring the band together as players and as people. "We just had to stay focused," Matt told *Uranium Music*, "there wasn't really any partying – just unload, play, load up and just drive forever. It was a lot of fun but painful work."[75]

"Again, you whore – again you do this to me!"

Trivium being Trivium, however, there was still a lot of room to enjoy life on the road, as Poggione recalls. "There was one time after a show when our merchandise guy was getting some action from this [girl] in the band van. She was so wasted, beyond wasted actually. The best thing about it was when the slut's husband found her having sex in the van – right in the act. He busted open the door and flipped out."

"He kept saying things like, 'I knew this was going happen,'" continues the bassist, "insanely shouting, 'Again, you whore – again you do this to me!' I had to stop him from trashing our van and starting fights by threatening him with two beer bottles. It was so funny because this guy was looking for his wife the entire night after the show and finally was pointed to the van by some fan in the parking lot."

"I also remember Matt and Travis getting in to a few drunken arguments about who was the most important member in the band," chuckles Poggione, "and they actually stopped driving one night at a tollstop to start a fight in the highway streets. I thought they were gonna get arrested for stopping in a public area to fight and argue about who was the more popular in the group!"

"Luckily, myself and the road crew got control of the situation just long enough to get past the police at the toll-stop and for them to bitch-fight each other in the hotel parking lot."

"Roadrunner gave them rock star status from the very beginning."

Aside from such shenanigans, however, it was an insight into how slick things could be on a major label. "The tour was fucking a great time for me personally," says Poggione, "it was beyond professional – it was fucking great to actually work in a major label production. Even though Trivium was an opening act at this time, Roadrunner gave them rock star status from the very beginning. It blew my mind to see the band all have cell phones going off at all times from different people in the industry and from their manager. I was very happy to travel around in a custom van and have a great hotel bed waiting for me each night. I ate like a pig and was treated very well during the entire tour – everything that I had asked for was given and provided without any hassle or a runaround!"

"We definitely were able to play for some of the people who wouldn't normally hear us."

Despite the shock at losing Young, the gigs – which also featured Beyond The Embrace as openers – were a good chance for Trivium to reach out to a new audience that may have found it difficult to find their recorded material in the shops.

"We definitely were able to play for some of the people who wouldn't normally hear us," commented Matt, "and on both tours nobody knew who we were, so yeah, it was great. I mean, people totally dug it on the Iced Earth tour, which was really cool."[76]

Reviews of the tour, however, were ambivalent, the media acknowledging that whilst Trivium had some talent, they weren't – yet – necessarily hitting the spot. Reviewer Randy of the German Metal 'zine *Daredevil* wasn't bowled over. "Trivium mix hardcore and newer In Flames-style thrash," he wrote of the Pittsburgh concert on May 12, "they have some great guitar melodies, and a confident stage presence, but I couldn't get past the clean vocals. The guy's screamed vocals are pretty strong, but his singing voice seemed a little whiney for my tastes. There was nothing wrong with the songwriting or performance; they definitely scored points for hanging out in the crowd for the other sets, and having ex-Monstrosity member Mike Poggione on bass."[77]

The bands were enjoying themselves, Tim 'Ripper' Owens of Iced Earth commenting on his official site that "the guys from Trivium and Beyond the Embrace are real cool and sounding great!"[78]

It had gone well with Poggione – onstage at least – prompting Heafy to comment slightly non-commitally that "he's very good – he totally has the stage presence. He dominated with that stuff, so that was great. We're still working out some stuff, so we'll see what's going to happen with him. He is incredible live."[79]

During the same interview, the songwriter revealed that the band was thinking of switching producers for their forthcoming Roadrunner album debut. "We're actually going to Andy Sneap for our next album," he said. "We were talking back and forth about who we were going to use, and he was one of the ideas for the next album. We came down to Sneap, and he has been one of my favourite producers forever so I'm excited to work with him. Jason definitely did help find our sound back in the early days."[80]

Trivium had, by now, utilised the downtime between live outings to write the vast majority of what was to become their new LP. "We wrote a big chunk of the record before we even signed to Roadrunner," said Corey, "the only time I think we had any pressure was when we had to write three songs in like three days before we had to go into the studio to do pre-production. But Roadrunner never put pressure on us, they just told us to do what we do best and write a Trivium album. So we just went in there and did what we wanted to do and it came out really good as far as we're concerned."[81]

The ambition and drive of the band once more showed a yearning to shift into a higher gear. And the bass issue needed to be resolved – once and for all. It wasn't just the music, there were acutely practical issues as well. "I was a few years older," explains Poggione "and had to look at things in a different manner… I had to make sure I could take care of my obligations." Naturally, like most people, Mike had bills to pay and needed to ensure that any commitment to Trivium was feasible for his position.

"They wanted someone more their age, and someone who had more similar tastes in music."

"They could not guarantee anything like that at the time and said it would take a few years to get their ball rolling regarding making profit and more income," he continues, "so I could not guarantee myself much at that time by staying with them."[82]

"But that's how the business goes – and I don't blame them… [ultimately] they wanted someone more their age, and someone who had more similar tastes in music."[83] It seems a shame, not least because Mike is one of the most colourful, entertaining and, lest we forget, talented bassists on the scene.

The search was back on for a bass player who could both rock it in the gig arena and, crucially, somebody who'd be available to focus solely on Trivium as his main musical outlet.

Jason Suecof's contacts and affability soon came up trumps once more. During June he had been working on a project with a group called Metal Militia. Whilst they were in Audiohammer laying some tracks down, Travis, Corey and Matt swooped down to the studio to hang out on an increasingly rare day off. They noticed that the band's bassist was technically superb, and a good, honest, funny guy who also shared their ambition and musical vision.

That bass player is Paolo Gregoletto, and he finally locked that revolving door of band members. "A few days [after the recording sessions in Audiohammer] we all got together to jam," Paolo later said, "and from the first song we played together I knew there was a musical chemistry between us."[84]

"I had lessons with the guy who was in The Commodores."

For the moment, however, the musical chemistry was secondary to an auspicious day in Trivium's career to date, as long-term supporters *Orlando Weekly* named them 'Band Of The Year 2004'.

"They released a great record – *Ember to Inferno* – late last year on a German label, and then, within the space of a few months, found themselves booked on tours with the likes of Iced Earth and Chimaira and ended up signed to Roadrunner Records," enthused the paper, "Like, that's a big deal. And, unlike some of Orlando's other nationally known 'heavy' bands, the gut-punching power metal that Trivium delivers is something to be proud of, as their combination of metal's heavy history and abundant technical proficiency results in something truly forward-looking and strong. Goes to show what happens when a band sets out to be 'good' rather than 'famous.'"[85]

Such local recognition was a real boost to the confidence of a group whose line-up was still lurching. Their career, however, was gathering pace, and it was announced that Trivium would take the road once more during August on the 'Road Rage Tour', alongside 3

Inches Of Blood (who later pulled out of the tour), Chimara and legends Machine Head.

Paolo Gregoletto was born on September 14, 1985 in Miami (population: fucking shitloads). In common with the other members of Trivium, he'd spent his time learning technique since first picking up his chosen instrument, taking bass lessons in order to ramp up his musical appreciation and technical skills.

"I had lessons with the guy who was in The Commodores," he told *Bass Guitar Magazine*'s Adrian Ashton, "so I learnt all about jazz and harmony and stuff. It was later on that I got into metal but it's helped me with my metal playing. I learnt how chord progressions worked, which you can then apply to any kind of music."[86]

As mentioned, Gregoletto had put those lessons to good use with a six-year stint as bassist and vocalist for the band, Metal Militia (named after the Metallica track). They were regulars on the South Florida gig circuit.

"I was doing my own shows at places like Daytona and Tampa,"[87] he recalled, "we had played shows together a few years back, and we kept in contact because they were in Orlando and I was in Ft. Lauderdale doing basically the same thing."

"Matt's dad managed them and my mom managed my band, and they kept in contact. When I found out they needed a bass player I decided I would go up and help them if they wanted. Eventually they wanted me to jam with them for a week while I was recording. I rehearsed with them for a few more weeks and learned all of their songs and went out on the Roadrage tour. Trivium is thrashier and faster [than Metal Militia]. Coming into it and playing the new stuff, when I saw it was fast, I was totally stoked, because that is the music I love."[88]

The Road Rage Tour was notable for many reasons; not only were the band rockin' it, they were also gigging alongside one of the bands with whom they'd always dreamed of playing. It was an opportunity that only Roadrunner could have offered, further validating their decision to sign with the company.[89]

The band were having a ball on the road, despite the cruelty of the weather, and Matt's regular tour missives to the Roadrunner website were drenched in his excitement and enthusiasm.

"At my favourite show so far [Worcester MA] people were dancing, moshing, pumping horns, screaming along with the songs. The energy was so intense I threw my guitar down during 'Pillars Of Serpents' to get a little more up close with our fans."[90]

"After the tour I came back home with hickies the size of welts all down my neck."

There are, of course, some, uh, 'fringe benefits' of being in a successful band. And with hormones raging, playing sizzling shows and rampant with youthful confidence, who wouldn't take advantage of such things? Heafy's mother was none too pleased when she saw the evidence, however, as he sheepishly admitted later to *Revolver* magazine. "After the tour I came back home with hickies the size of welts all down my neck. My mom saw them, and she wouldn't speak to me for two days!"[91]

The aforementioned inclement weather was actually the forceful and unforgiving Hurricane Charlie, which tragically decimated much of their home state. Trivium being Trivium, however, were determined to see their gigs through.

When they were in Atlanta, Georgia, they heard the hurricane was about to hit Florida, right in the path of their route for the next show in Orlando. Their reaction?

"Man! We haven't played Orlando in a long time! No!" Travis was even more determined: "I don't give a fuck, I'll drive."

"We'd been out for a long time and I just really wanted to get home," said Travis, "my whole plan was to play the show, then sleep in my own bed. I just got behind the wheel and said, 'we're gonna do this, so get in, and here we go.'"[92] "The next day," said Corey, "on the way to the venue, it looked like the city had been bombed."[93] They all agreed it was one of the best shows of the tour."[94]

The reaction was promising from the media this time. "As far as stage presence and chops are concerned, the quartet was top notch," said a reviewer who'd caught the gig in Laurence, Kansas on August 27, "lead singer/guitarist Matt Heafy never let the crowd catch a breath and put his heart and soul into the performance. The style, dubbed deathcore by the band, is more thrash than anything else, mixed with a helping of hardcore. The riffs were blazing and the soloing surprisingly accomplished given the youth of the members."[95]

In a curious way, that aforementioned hurricane and through-the-night drive had brought the band even closer together. After all, if you can spend ten or more hours in a cramped van being buffeted by horror-movie weather, not knowing whether you're gonna make it through to the other side; if you can close your nostrils to the farts and the sweat of musicians who've been on the road for weeks; if you can keep your humour whilst the insults and the piss-takes swirl around; if you can curl up and sleep on stifling, sticky seats; if you can do all of this and still hang loose with a bassist you barely know *and still* get on famously, then, darn-it, things are looking pretty good."[96]

It's also pretty tempting to consider that hurricane as a powerful metaphor for the career of Trivium up to this point: battered and bruised from all sides, sure, but driving through the eye of the storm with a determination that they would come out the other side all the stronger. In short, they'd survived the worst that could be thrown at them, and from hereon in the future was surely to be even brighter. Losing Brent Young may have brought the dark clouds, but gaining Gregoletto turned out to be a ray of light in the wider context. "It was really meant to be with him,"[97] was how Travis simply summed up Paolo's arrival.

"What's really strange, being that none of us really grew up together, is that we all basically have the same fucking background story, our favourite bands are all the same bands, the first song we each rehearsed with was 'For Whom The Bell Tolls.' Little things like that just make it seem like it was supposed to happen."[98]

Such matters were, thankfully, now firmly in the past. Paolo was perfect, to the point where he actually left Metal Militia to concentrate on Trivium full-time.[99] With a stable line-up, a growing set-list, an ever-more powerful live show and a crunchy confidence to boot, it was a happy, battle-hardened Trivium that approached the studio that September.

7

ascendancy

On September 13, 2004, Trivium hit Morrisound Studios in Tampa to lay down the drum tracks for the new material. By this point, the initial plans to use Andy Sneap for the whole recording had evolved into a decision to work again on the tracking of the music with Jason Suecof – with whom they'd been in pre-production since June – the subsequent mixing and mastering to take place in Sneap's Backstage Studios in Derbyshire, UK. Suecof's innate musicianship, personality and familiarity with the band's sonic and musical ambitions had proved to be just too much to throw away.

"Jason can definitely be considered as the fifth member of Trivium,"[100] says Stefan Luedicke, "he's spent more time with the band than anybody else and has a huge influence on the band's sound. He's an amazing producer and Trivium would probably not be the same band as they are now [without him]."

"We sat there for hour on hour every day," said Matt, "even when I was on the road, taking notes on what was not good, and what harmonies needed to be used here and there. It's really studying the raw song and perfecting it."[101]

The hurricanes continued to follow the group around Florida, but it didn't seem to bother the boys any, Matt commenting that the drums were sounding "crisp and heavy as hell."[102]

The sessions for Trivium's Roadrunner debut were going swimmingly, marking also the first recordings of songs that had been written in conjunction with other band members, with Corey co-authoring several of the tracks. Paolo's introduction to the group was at too late a stage for any similar involvement, as the metallers had been writing material constantly in the downtime before – and after – signing to Lifeforce.

"It wasn't just me 100% writing the guitar parts, it was back and forth between Corey and I," explained Matt. "It wasn't really a drastic change; with Trivium we always write songs the same: we let the song write itself. I never really go into it thinking a specific way of thinking the way a song should be. It's always been a natural process and it's still the same way. The same way we've always done it."[103]

The album – to be called *Ascendancy* – once more marks a massive step ahead of what had come previously; sonically, its ferocity is boosted by a production that both polishes the tracks and blasts the album's narrative ever higher. Beaulieu and Heafy's twin guitar assault, after a year of playing together, has begun to take on a life all of its own. Whilst individually they're both technically adept and fiery, together there's an intangible invention about the

Where it all began:
DIY Records, 2000. *Toby Brown*

DIY Records' hi-tech booking
system, 2000. *Toby Brown*

Brent, Travis and Matt – moody early shot, 2002. *Killer Camera*

Guy in Stonesour T-shirt wonders if he left oven on, Trivium rock regardless: Orlando Metal Awards 2003. *Killer Camera*

I can do this in my sleep:
Matt at Orlando Metal Awards 2002.
Killer Camera

Dad Rock: Brian accepts his son's 'Best Guitarist Gong', Orlando Metal Awards 2002. *Killer Camera*

Flyer for 2003 Orlando Metal Awards.
Matt Wagner

So fast he needs eight sticks:
Travis at Orlando Metal Awards 2003.
Killer Camera

Alex Vieira (Right) finds hole in pocket on trip with Jason Suecof (Left)
and Matt Heafy (Centre), 2004. *Alex Vieira*

'Ain't they got no barbers where
you come from boy?' Brent Young
at Orlando Metal Awards 2003.
Killer Camera

Matt returns to the land of
his birth, 2006. *Yuka Hirose*

Trivium Flyers. *Matt Wagner*

'Ember And The Infernos' fool a total of no people whatsoever – London Islington Academy, March 22 2006. *Karen Toftera www.shotonstage.com*

Matt and mates edge away from Mike Poggione. Only known shot
of Trivium with their temporary bass player, May 2004. *Mike Poggione*

Kerrang-tastic! *Brian Rasic / Rex Features*

Matt with the band Mindscar, 2001.

Ritchie Brown

---(we will rock you)---
(INTRO) The End Of Everything---
Like Light To The Flies
Rain
Suffocating sight

Washing Away Me In The Tides
The Deceived (to middle/ clapping)
A Gunshot To The Head Of Trepidation

(BLACKOUT/ guitar change)

---(INTERLUDE) Ashes---
To Burn The Eye
Ember To Inferno (Corey Sings All)
Requiem

(guitar change)

Drum Solo
Travis/ Paolo/ Corey Solo
Travis/ Paolo/ Matt Solo
Corey vs. Matt Duel
Corey + Matt – Brokeback Mountain

Ascendancy
Drowned And Torn Asunder
Declaration (Dom/ Walk)

Dying In Your Arms
(fake ender . . . encore)
Pull Harder On The Strings Of Your Martyr
(horns and holmeism)

The song never remains the same…
Trivium set list, late 2005.

Karen Toftera www.shotonstage.com

Paolo in full flow at Download,
June 2006.

Karen Toftera www.shotonstage.com

'SCREAM FOR ME DONINGTONNNN!':
Heafy rocks Download, 2006.

Karen Toftera www.shotonstage.com

Edible microphone tastes terrible: Matt at Wolverhampton's Wulfrun Hall,
September 19, 2005. *Dan, Satan's FishTank*

way the players weave and prowl around each other that is at once edgy and emotive.[104]

"Having a good second guitar for us was totally crucial," Matt told Bob Gulla of *Guitar One*, "now we can duel, trade off, harmonise, and everything else you can think of."

"Corey is my cohort in evil."

Beaulieu agreed: "It knocks the door open. Matt used to play power chords and sing the melody on his own; now you've got the power chords, the vocal melody, and the guitar melody all working together."[105]

"Corey is my cohort in evil," cackled Matt, "his style is such a throwback to 80s styling. It's fast, flashy and cool, and that's something you don't really hear these days."[106] The sound – and the band – had matured since *Ember To Inferno* was written, never mind recorded, and the new album reflected all the struggles they'd been through to reach this point, as well as a shiny confidence that spoke of great things to come.

Opening once more with a piano-based and gothy introduction, 'The End Of Everything', when the first band track 'Rain' kicks in it's with an enormous flash of harmonic guitar work that develops into the multi-grade thrash and crunch that was becoming the band's signature. It's four minutes packed with more riffs, breakdowns, contrasts and creative work than many lesser bands *can't* shoehorn into a whole career. Depending on how you look at it, the group is either putting down a marker that screams: "we're back", or announcing their arrival to the world. Possibly both are true.

The Cozy Powell-like blasting drum intro to 'Pull Harder On The Strings Of Your Martyr' drives the track –

and the album – into top gear, with Heafy and Gregoletto growling and scratching at the eyes of the listener from the inside atop, before launching into stunning Maiden-ist breakdowns, pinch harmonics and chugging Machine Head-esque aggression. The solos here – as throughout the LP - are superior and brutal in their mélange of technical ability and personality.

'Drowned And Torn Asunder', the über-catchy, double-drum demonisms of the title track itself, and the mighty future-classic 'A Gunshot To The Head Of Trepidation' (of which more later) tighten the tension, the tunefulness and the tremulous sonic shimmer even further; and we're not even halfway through the LP.

The extremely anthemic track 'Like Light To The Flies' flashes toward the relatively laid-back but melodic 'Dying In Your Arms' – which is reminiscent of Jimmy Eat World and very different from the rest of the album, as Matt explained.

"We just wanted to do something different," he told *Power Play*, "it wasn't like we set out to do a pop song or a song for college radio. I wanted to do our 'Fade To Black', you know? I wanted to get a bit more of a diverse sound on the album, stretch ourselves a bit."[107]

It quickly blasts back into the Metallica-esque 'The Deceived' as the tracks keep firing at the listener in an assault of classic metal infused with a growing, bloody claw that rips the beating heart out of a – gasp – pop sensibility and couches it in a distorted diorama of metal class. 'Suffocating Sight' (though the cheesy B-movie keyboards are frankly horrendous) and 'Departure' whack the LP right back into the realms of tuneful-chorus, 100mph riff-n-shred and primal scrawlings.

"Lyrically," explained Heafy of 'Departure', "that song deals with depression leading into suicide, basically feeling that the whole world is giving up on you and losing all faith. I've never been suicidal, but it's there to give comfort to people who really do feel that way and just show them that someone else has felt that way, and it's possible to get through it – just knowing that there can be a positive outcome."[108]

It all comes to an end with the epic energy, effected vocals, Prodigy-snaffled riffery and driving narrative of 'Declaration', which Matt later described as his favourite track on the LP. "It's so everywhere, and shows everything we can do in a seven minute song, so it's never boring."[109]

"Making this album was really cool and fun process."

Ascendancy is, all in all, an album which is full of life and death, gristle and smoothness, roar and release; crucially, it's a set of songs that have been planned, thought out, arranged and developed to full effect. And at the core of it is the feeling that, contrary to the metalcore tag with which people were seeking to label them, Trivium was purely and simply a *metal* act. Sure, they take influence from everything around them – that is the human condition – but the overriding feeling is of a release that is both of its time and outside time.

Travis had enjoyed the space to stretch out that the added time in the studio had afforded. "Making this album was really cool and fun process," he said, "we got a chance to do a lot of stuff that we hadn't been able to do before – like pre-production."[110] Their impressively supportive label never rushed them, giving them about a month to track it and a month for the mixing and mastering, making it an altogether more relaxed process.

Lyrically, the themes that the album explores are both dark and ambitious, as Heafy explained, "[it covers] spousal abuse, broken homes and child abuse. It's stuff I've always just been extremely opposed to and I just felt the need to make others aware."[111]

Matt also revealed the breadth of their influences: "When I wrote 'Declaration' – the fastest song we've done – I was only listening to emo. It's weird. I decided that if you listen to something completely different, something that you cannot draw an influence from, you'll write the most original music possible – nothing that can be accidentally ripped off and filtered into your brain."[112]

"Ascendancy is a personal statement about the band."

In the same manner that calling their Lifeforce LP *Ember To Inferno* implied the lighting of the rampant fires of roaring success for Trivium, the new album title was also rippling with resonance.

"*Ascendancy* is a personal statement about the band," explained Matt, "having to gradually ascend in the scene, in the music scene in general, and in our lives; it became a bigger thing, a bigger entity. The word *ascendancy* means to have higher power, domination over everything else, I figured it was just cool as an album title as it's also a personal statement."[113]

"It's kinda how we feel as a band," agreed Corey, "we want to be the most dominating, biggest band in the world. It definitely fits the music. Why be in something if you don't want to be the best? That's kinda our goal: work hard and be the biggest band we can be."[114]

Whilst the group busied themselves with cool song and album titles and studio work, their record label were also preparing an edit of the 'Like Light To The Flies' video, which the group had shot way back in January 2004. But the version that hit MTV2's *Headbangers' Ball Volume 2* on September 25 was very different to Dale Resteghini's boy-and-girl-meets-spooky-castle, girl-comes-to-a-gruesome-implied-end horror epic that had led directly to the band being signed by Roadrunner in the first instance.

"I think Roadrunner felt like it was too graphic," muses Resteghini, "which it wasn't. The guy [in the video] at that time was a VJ on Fuse. He's known as Dennis The Menace. He's a black guy, also a rapper. We don't even say that they're boyfriend and girlfriend, we see that they're together. We actually initially had one of the guys from Mudvayne who were meant to be in it — but they had to back out at the last minute. We needed a replacement, so it was just a nice big extra bonus to have a VJ on a brand new band's debut video. But the version that people have seen is only a performance video. Ultimately they didn't show that video, but I still have it on my video reel."

"It's really weird to see my face on TV,"

Regardless, the re-edited video does show off the force of Trivium to the world, and it was subsequently hitting the airwaves left, right and centre, including its debut on the influential Metal Injection online TV station on October 2.

"It's really weird to see my face on TV," mused Matt, "it hasn't really clicked that we've done all this touring and people know who we are. We are all humble guys and are really appreciative of everything, so it's all very mind-blowing."[115]

In keeping with Matt and the band's realisation of the importance of a convergent aesthetic to all they do, they began to look for a suitable cover artist. And it was Heafy who hit upon the ideal person with whom to work.

101

"I was just browsing through this record store," recalled Matt to Mark Freestone of *Power Play*, "and I found this Mastodon album, *Remission*. I saw the artwork on the cover and thought 'These guys must be huge, how come I haven't heard of them before?' So even though I got into Mastodon off the album's music, I had to get this guy Paul [Romano] to do the artwork for *Ascendancy*."[116]

The cover features a mummy-esque cousin of Iron Maiden's Eddie rising into a volcanic sky; very 1980s, very metal, and very Trivium. "Pretty much all we did was we gave Paul a copy of the lyrics and a basic concept," continued Corey, "he read the lyrics and got an idea of what we were looking for."[117]

With the artwork sorted, and finishing touches being put to the vocal recording, it was time to score some new promo photos, as freelance shootist Josh Rothstein recalled in an interview for this book.

"When I got there they were doing their vocals and it was kinda the end of their album," he says. "Roadrunner sent me down cause they know I have a specific way I like to shoot, which is a more organic thing. The locations that I get have an aged look to them, and they talked to the band. They said 'Look dude, just do what you do, with us. We like your style of keeping it real; we'll listen to you, you just gotta give it some direction.'"

"Which is really cool, cause I think it's kinda hard sometimes for a band to admit that they're willing to give up that kind of [power]. That is a maturity, to say 'Just go ahead and do what you think – just give us some direction and we're willing to go for the ride.'"

"The day before, I went out location scouting with Travis and his good friend," continues Rothstein. "I'd met the other guys – to say hello to them – at the studio. That night, we all went out for dinner before the shoot. And we had a nice meal, and we ended up seeing Team

America – one of the most underrated films of our generation. We were all freaking out over that film, we were laughing our asses off! So the next day on the shoot was all Team America references. You know, like 'Come over here and get on your knees!' All that shit in the film. It was fucking hilarious."

"Because these guys were already quite popular down in Florida when I was shooting them, they could have had the attitude, like, 'Fuck you, some hot shot New York photographer, why should we listen to you?' But they didn't."

"Come over here and get on your knees!"

"It was right on the brink, there was a good buzz about them. They started to get some really good feedback on what they were doing, their sound and everything, and I think they knew that the photoshoot was gonna be really important. I don't think they'd done an extensive shoot like this. I had a makeup artist, and a stylist, really did it to the nines. And they were up for everything… they were really amenable to letting things happen with the shoot. They did seem like they were poised to do what they had to do, to be successful."

Rothstein also recalls the family atmosphere that permeated and defined how incredibly tight all in, uh, Team Trivium, had become. "We went to their house at one point," remembers the photographer. "Matt was living at home with his parents. Corey and Paolo were living in the house with Matt – with the family! I just thought that was really cool, cause usually at that age, and with that type of music, sometimes you have this very kinda anti-establishment, fuck-you to your parents type of thing. But Matt's dad is this big strong dude who's very encouraging of this whole thing. His mother's Asian, and she's this really sweet woman who helped mend some of his clothes for him. A really sweet family. You have to have that support."

With the definitive photos now in place, Trivium headed over the Atlantic for mixing and mastering sessions with Andy Sneap, something of a legend in metal and rock circles for his work with acts including Machine Head, Testament and Obituary. Whilst the group busied themselves discovering the dubious delights of warm ale and soggy chips[118], Sneap's mates buzzed about the studio, dropping in to listen in on the music by this crazy new band of American metallers.

"The pub was full of old MILFs that were fussing over the two lads being all fresh with American accents!"

Gizz Butt, guitarist for The Prodigy and now shredding it to the max with the band The More I See, recalled it well when he spoke to me for this book. "Andy gave me a call one day and told me he had this band in the studio, and that Roadrunner had really big hopes for them," chuckles the man who has a personally designed seven-string guitar line for Ibanez: "It was the first I'd heard of them! Andy's one of my best mates – he invites me up to the studio a lot. We chill out with the bands, have a few drinks in the local pubs, go back to the studio and Andy gives us a tour of his latest gadgets, then we play a few games, watch videos and take the rise out of Andy's girlfriend Helen."

"Andy had talked to the Trivium guys about The More I See," continues Butt, "and they all seemed into the idea of having a boozy session as it was the end of their mix. I asked the others if they wanted to come along but they were busy sacrificing bats – apart from Chad who was bang up for it. We went down to an old pub in Belper – it was pretty cold at the time. This pub had a log fire so we loved it but it was hardly pre-rock club material. We had a great laugh with Matt and Travis, who were beaming from ear to ear as they'd been listening to near final mixes of their tracks. The pub was full of old MILFs that were fussing over the two lads being all fresh with American accents!"

Such bonding sessions inevitably end up in collaborations, and thus Gizz Butt and TMIS compadre Chad Sutherland ended up lending their drunken shouts to the immensely powerful breakdown in the middle of 'A Gunshot To The Head Of Trepidation', which was destined to become one of the most popular audience-participation tracks in Trivium's set.

Hangovers in hand, head and breadbasket, the multimedia-savvy Trivium spent the rest of November 2004 setting up their own myspace account so that their growing number of fans could communicate directly with them in as many ways as possible, before heading out on the road that was becoming their home for well-received US dates alongside No Warning and the mighty Fear Factory, as well as an appearance alongside Killswitch Engage. As the year ended, the quartet's activities had accelerated even more, bringing purpose, validation and excitement to what was rapidly becoming a band with the ability to switch through the gears all the way up to 11. December brought no respite from the pace, with three pre-Christmas tour dates just as Santa was ready to empty his bulging sack and come down chimneys across the world. This time, Trivium was on a bill with Ill Niño, 40 Below Summer and, ironically, George Moore's band The Autumn Offering.

More and more people were getting to hear first-hand what these four young metallers that everyone was whispering about, actually sounded like. More and more people were beginning to get on board with the new force in metal. Scintillating live dates were becoming the norm, and the days of playing in a sweaty rehearsal space for eight hours a day, frustrated at the lack of gig opportunities, were way behind the group.

But those people who saw the band during a fantastic year for Trivium were to prove a mere drop in the ocean. The triumphs of 2004 were many, but even those giant strides were to pale into the greying and destitute distance in comparison to the astonishing times that 2005 had in store.

8

Declarations
of intent

" **I** think that ever since Day One our goal has been to be The New Metallica. Ever since I joined the band the drive to grab that goal never fell through."[119]

Matthew Kiichi Heafy, in many interviews over the years – including the above sound-bite he offered *New York Metro* on January 7, 2005 – has not faltered from his avowed aim. From the first belligerent bashings alongside Travis, Jarred Bonaparte and Brad Lewter, through the subsequent years of struggle to find permanent members; through the yearning to find a suitable deal; through the ever-more-confident writing and performing of ever-more-complex songs – the eyes remained fixed hard on the prize.

Of course, Metallica's career has been massively influential; without them Trivium – and countless other bands of varying quality – would never have existed. But Heafy's [and his band mates'] continually confident statement of intent runs slightly deeper than a superficial, copyist, fan-boy approach. To be The New Metallica doesn't mean being *like* Metallica. It means *having the same impact* as Metallica. To inspire, to bring forth quality of metal, to rock honest and true and to strive to start up a new wave of bands who may one day stand aside you. This is a very important – nay vital – distinction; a distinction which many have chosen to ignore in favour of a reactionary, hackles-raised opportunity to snarl back about these cheeky American youngsters, still wet behind the goddamn ears. It can be taken as a kinda insouciant cockiness that's got up the nose of more than one journalist and not a few metallers, sending them into paroxysms of spluttering rage. As the band's profile soared during 2005, the naysayers reached a frenzy of irritation on occasion, as we shall shortly see.

"It's inevitable that they will blow up this year."

In the meantime, there was the small matter of developing a career. Roadrunner made 'Pull Harder On The Strings Of Your Martyr' available as a download single on January 10, a taster for *Ascendancy* – rapidly becoming one of the most eagerly-anticipated albums since… well, since You Know Who. Trivium, meanwhile, got back on the road for a series of dates during January alongside It Dies Today, The Acacia Strain and All that Remains.

"Their thrashy take on the popular US metal sound easily puts them up there with God Forbid and Shadows

Fall," wrote one reviewer who caught the tour, "and it's inevitable that they will blow up this year."[120]

With the live shows going great, the news filtered through that Trivium was a candidate to join the forthcoming Ozzfest 2005 tour. Votes were cast on the Ozzfest website – and later the Floridians found, to their delight, that they had, indeed, been selected to perform on the travelling metal circus that summer. A nice surprise, maybe, but hardly a shock; the buzz about the new album was reaching far and wide, with the first advance copies of the LP filtering out to the eager media. The band were 'Featured Artist Of The Week' on the influential UK rock station, *Extreme Radio*, and all of the metal magazines were starting to request media access to the band, particularly in Great Britain.

An interesting distraction for the group happened pretty much off the cuff on January 22, when they found themselves back in Florida for the first time since the previous year, rehearsing at the Classic Cases store in Sanford. Inviting mates, street teamers and a selected audience down for a barbeque, a couple of beers and – if there was time amidst the (delayed) Saturnalia – some music, the band roared through the *Ascendancy* album in its entirety for the first time. It was a low-key gig (if it can even be classed as such), but an enjoyable one that both relaxed the band and brought them back in contact with the people who were working so hard for them in spreading the word at ground level. It also allowed them to hook up with old friends who they hadn't seen for a while thanks to their new life as road monsters. With dates starting to be finalised for another high profile tour – this time alongside Kataklysm and behemoths Danzig – it was to be the last time for a while that the band were to have an opportunity to relax in such a setting and, as it was only four days prior to Matt Heafy's nineteenth birthday, it was a double celebration.

On January 30, Trivium travelled to New York to hook up once more with Dale 'Rage' Resteghini, this time to shoot a video for their single, 'Pull Harder On The Strings Of Your Martyr'.

"For 'Pull Harder...' we actually wanted to go with more of a narrative but the label said they just wanted to give a hard performance," explains Resteghini, "so I came up with the idea of dressing the entire stage with sheets of aluminium to make it look very Old School Metal. And that came out great. We put a character in there to be the artist who created the mural – which was the artwork that they used to market the entire record."

"A lot of times in videos for me it's not about the end result," he continues, "it's how you get there. And I wanted to pay homage to the old Tool and Metallica videos where there was this abstract character, just in a nondescript place, doing all kinds of crazy things. And it was kinda cool at the end just to see what he created."

Some kind of monster, perhaps? Regardless, Trivium continued to clock up the road miles, backing Dillinger Escape Plan in February. "That was probably the worst tour we could have done," Matt mused later, "it just didn't work with us because people wanted a really technical band and we're a metal band so there's a difference. That was the tour that didn't work."[121]

Not all the feedback was positive in their home country, either, with *Decibel Magazine*'s review of the Hamilton Underground gig on February 4 merely commenting that, "as for thrashers Trivium, well, their frontman can only be hurting his larynx with his litany of embarrassing stage raps."[122]

Putting yourself onstage is to put your head above the parapet; playing high profile tours is to expose yourself to critical barbs (and occasionally critical barbarism). It is the nature of the beast. Critics are many, and it's often easier to be negative than it is to hook up with a new energy and strive to understand it. Criticism, and especially music criticism, like any kind of artistic endeavour, is an entirely subjective process – it's a symbiotic relationship as well as a double-edged sword: bands thrive on media coverage, and the media needs bands to write about. But as a new day dawns, a new magazine deadline approaches, or another gig is scheduled, the previous day's words and deeds are dead and gone, forgotten forever and only of use as today's chip wrappers.[123] And, so, undaunted by mere reviews, but fuelled by the future-rush, Trivium completed that month heading up to Toronto to hook up with the Danzig tour, where they had the dubious – and difficult – task of opening up to an audience predominately there to watch their heroes headline. But such is the bread of a rising band, and ever has it been so.[124]

"That was probably the worst tour we could have done."

"It was pretty much playing to Danzig's crowd," conceded Corey, "we were opening for him and our record hadn't come out yet... We still had a couple of shows with fans and stuff like that – and we definitely made some new fans."[125]

"It was crazy, the shows were incredible," said Travis, "his band's great – we love Danzig and it was a lot of fun. We didn't really get to see Danzig too much – he kinda sticks to himself and stays on his bus – but he came out one night and watched our set, and then met us backstage and told us it was a good job, and he was happy to have us on the tour. We hung out with the rest of the band."[126]

The album, meanwhile, continued to gather momentum. Radio-wise, CMJ Loud Rock and CMJ

Spins both put it at No. 1 in their charts, whilst FMQB had it at No. 3. Initial album reviews were beginning to trickle in; the first drops to dribble through a crack in a dam behind which hundreds of thousands of tonnes of power were pushing for release.

"My first impression from this CD was that it was actually 'heavier' than the last record," wrote *Metal Rage*, "not heavier as if they put blastbeats in songs, but more focussed on crushing riffs, and tighter drumming as well. The band has clearly improved themselves as musicians. Heafy's vocals sound much better, and it seems that he has found his voice."[127] *Hard Beat* magazine, meanwhile, felt it was a "scorching sophomore effort" and a "modern metal landscape of sound that's hook-filled, powerful and razor-sharp."[128]

"When compared to the current trend of music, namely, post-hardcore," wrote *East Coast Romper*, "this group is the idyllic antithesis. From the speedy thrash rhythms to the crushing double bass assaults, Trivium is stating their case for music that is innovative in its approach and pattern."

"This is something that can get huge beyond control."

"Rounding out this potpourri of noise is the occasional lead that seemed to always be in the right place and the right time – not forced for the sake of sounding unique," continued the reviewer, "the vocal range between the growls that own the verses and the striking vocals that control the choruses further adds to an already impressive array of intelligently written music. There is no need to single out any song, because, from top to bottom, the whole disc is amazingly constructed and is, without a shadow of a doubt, the best album of 2005 to surface so far."[129]

Long-term supporters *Pitriff* enthused about "the resurgence of American metal," commenting that *Ascendancy* was "a powerful statement that should put this band on the map," rating the album nine out of ten; *Live4Metal* took it a step further, saying that "this is perhaps a band head and shoulders above almost any of their peers," in a review that also named Trivium as being capable of "possibly the biggest breakthrough story since Pantera," and concluding that "*Ascendancy* is undoubtedly the enthralling soundtrack to one of the most promising and talented metal acts that the world has seen this side of the millennium. If there's any justice left in this world of ours, then this is irrefutably a band destined for the type of fame and success that few others will ever experience."[130] Dutch webzine *Lords Of Metal* agreed, warning that "this is something that can get huge beyond control."[131]

The band appeared to be getting under the skin of their US press compatriots – another reviewer predicting that "*Ascendancy* is going to the claim this year's 'Best Metal Album' and in my opinion 'Best Album.' Trivium is going to engrave their name in the wall of metal and if they decided to stop after this album, *Ascendancy* would live on for years to come."[132]

Stop?

The band had hardly started to show what they could do, and March saw the latest Roadrage tour – Trivium on a rotating headline bill alongside 3 Inches Of Blood, The Agony Scene and Still Remains. For Trivium, the tour served both to support the release of the Trivium LP as well as celebrating Roadrunner Records' 25th Anniversary. The US dates during March went exceptionally well – when they opened up at 8pm at Detroit's Harpo's Venue on March 5, the crowd was already chanting their name at full voice. Charged to the max, the band didn't disappoint, the set culminating with Matt diving into the sprawling mosh-pit during 'Pull Harder...'. The band was having a ball, on and off the stage – that is, until they hit Still Remains's home town of Grand Rapids, Michigan.

"We offered to pay them but they were all being jerks."

"We were in the fourth show of the tour," explained Corey, "and right when we got there, right outside the city – maybe ten minutes away – we stopped at a gas station. As soon as we turned the van on, it started making this weird noise and stuff, like the belts being funny, and stuff like that." They played that night's show then took the van to a garage. Assuming any repair might be swift, they headed off to an internet café to post yet another highly entertaining tour missive. "We went out and got something to eat, you know, we figured, 'kill two hours, we won't be late.'"[133]; "Goddamn," wrote Matt, "have the crowds been showing love, metal, and goddamn insanity! I love it."[134] On their return to the garage however, they were shocked to be told their van would be grounded for several days.

Gutted and with the next show in Cleveland evaporating in front of their eyes, they were then left with no option but to drive from Grand Rapids to New York after they had picked up the repaired van. However, this didn't get done until around noon so with a twelve hour drive to the Big Apple, the band had virtually no chance of making the show. Worse still, Roadrunner had set up a fantastic night in celebration of the label's 25th anniversary, ramming the venue with media, fans, record business players and generally important faces. Trivium could not have picked a worse show to miss… "So we end up telling them we're not going to make it, we're not going to get there until at least one in the morning."[135]

Once again Roadrunner flexed its supportive muscles and actually got straight on the phone and booked the band an internal flight; yet they were still not home and dry. When they got to the airport, their flight was delayed over two hours. Panic levels rising, Trivium got in the standby queue for an express flight and, with sweat gathering, were delighted to find that enough passengers had not turned up to get the crew and band on board. Except for two roadies who had the unenviable task of driving the repaired van all the way to New York on their own!

Yet the nightmare was not over. "Then when we get to New York," Matt continues, "there was a mile long line for cabs, and we asked everyone to let us go first. We offered to pay them but they were all being jerks. Finally, this nice guy let us pay him and take his cab, and as soon as we get to the venue, we walked in the door, went up on stage and performed! It was a really bad three days, definitely the most intense ones while we've been touring so far."[136]

It was also an opportunity for the road crew to earn their corn, as Corey laughed. "A couple of our tour guys made the long haul of driving the van and the trailer all the way to New York!"[137]

Road Rage indeed.

Still, Trivium's growing love for the rock 'n' roll lifestyle was undimmed – even if their stamina wasn't quite up to the mark – as Corey explained to *Metal Underground*.

"We played CBGB's, and after the show they had an open bar," he laughed, "you know, everyone in a metal band, you can't turn down free alcohol like that, especially in a bar. So, me and two of the guys from my band took a lengthy cab drive from the venue to Jersey City. I can say

I was the most sober of them and Paolo, our bassist, was completely wasted." Puke ensued.

"We had our equipment in the trunk and we got to the hotel and he wouldn't give us our stuff back until we gave him extra money to clean up the cab," continued Corey, "Paolo said he'd pay since it was his fault; he roamed around looking for an ATM that wasn't there, and wound up walking into the glass door of the fucking hotel. So I ended up paying the cab driver, plus toll and the money to clean his cab, gave him 100 dollars just to get our equipment back from him!"[138]

Legendary UK metal magazine *Kerrang!* had been at the gig, and thought that headliners Trivium "with their juddering riffage, Maiden-esque leads and screamo-style vocals probably represent the most brazen face of post-Killswitch metal tonight, had a tough job following the metal maniacs preceding them onstage. Despite imparting a mellower tone, they capped the night in grand style, however, and thanks to their savvy mix of might and melody, look all set to light a considerable fire under the arses of the likes of Atreyu and Avenged Sevenfold."[139]

The only bit of insurmountably bad news, in truth, to beset the band in the early months of 2005 was the announcement that they'd had to pull out of several dates that had been planned as support to labelmates Slipknot on their Subliminal Verses tour during April; time constraints being cited as the factor. It was a disappointment, for sure, but the sheer pace of events meant that there was little time for moping after such matters.

The influential internet TV station *Music Choice* presented the LP in its entirety on March 6 in an item called 'Trivium: Declassified'. It was an hour-long special, with staggered show times and repeats running throughout the day, the music interspersed with interviews with band members about the album and the current status of activities in Team Trivium and information about the Road Rage Tour. *Fuse* accepted the video for 'Pull Harder On The Strings Of Your Martyr' on its Uranium show, beginning to air it to the TV watching public on March 14, and MTV2's *Headbangers' Ball* show grabbed the video for debut five days later.

Ascendancy was released on March 14, 2005 in the UK, a day later in America. Its accolades came thick and fast; the album debuted at Number 4 in *Billboard*'s Heatseekers Chart for new music, Number 21 in the Hard Rock charts, and Number 151 in the Top 200 albums. Elsewhere, the venerable *New York Times* made it a 'Critics' Pick', *Guitar One* Magazine made Brian Heafy's early advertising spend more than worthwhile by naming the band as 'Breakthrough Artist' and the legendary *Alternative Press* advised its readers that Trivium was one of '100 Bands You Need To Know'. The LP had by this stage also clocked up five straight weeks at Number 1 in both College and Hard Rock radio. It reached Number 8 in the UK Rock Chart and debuted at Number 113 in the full chart; listeners and buyers raised on NWOBHM were getting on board with the band rather quicker than their American counterparts. First week sales of 7,048, in fact, were the fourth best-selling in Roadrunner's history.

Trivium celebrated with a raucous appearance at the Industry shindig South-By-Southwest in Austin, Texas. SXSW, as it's known, is a haven for A&R scouts, press and radio people from all over the world who converge there to network, get pissed, chow down on free food and occasionally actually catch the odd live show. Many bands over the years have launched careers with well-received gigs at the conference, and it had come at a perfect time for Trivium.

Corey, as usual, was a happy bunny. "The tour is going great," he offered, "the last couple shows in Texas were sick – those Texans know how to rock! All you lady Trivium fans need to get your butts to a show and come party with us!"[140]

The UK press were beginning to whip themselves up into a foaming frenzy with weekly magazine *Kerrang!* rating the album KKKK, reviewer Nick Young commenting that, "as 18-year-old frontman Matt Heafy ('Best Metal Guitarist' at Orlando's 2002 Metal Awards, apparently) flits between deathly bellows and uplifting choruses, while widdling his way into oblivion and back for 'A Gunshot To The Head Of Trepidation', you start to unravel the sheer quantity of groove and ferocity these four Floridians are capable of. Complete with orchestral intro, duel guitar harmonies, and lightning-speed fretwork, this is power incarnate."[141]

Power Play was similarly impressed. "From the gorgeous artwork by Paul Romano," wrote Mark Freestone, "to the last note of 'Declaration', this album oozes quality from every fibre to every digit. Truly a stunning album and a complete package. Drop your preconceptions, see past the hardcore vocals and drink up the liquid metal."[142]

The mighty *Metal Hammer*, the leading UK monthly metal and rock rag, were immediately on board. "*Ascendancy* draws on many influences, which are so brilliantly applied that it never sounds derivative," raved reviewer Brian Magill, "in fact, such is the quality on offer here that Trivium breathe new life into genres that you thought had nowhere left to go. Scandinavian thrash, NWOBHM, metalcore – it's all here, cohesively updated and revitalized for the 21st century."[143]

"Executed brilliantly," mused Darren Sadler of the respected monthly UK magazine *Rock Sound*, "these Floridians are a true class act and with youth on their side, they could well be set for great things."[144]

April began with the UK magazine *Total Guitar* featuring the band in their 'Monitor' section, and reaffirming that the band were capable of being 'The Next Metallica'. Trivium would have a chance to prove themselves on the 10th Anniversary Ozzfest tour beginning on July 15, with the line-up officially announced on March 16. The rolling festival was to be headlined by Black Sabbath and Iron Maiden; a match made in heaven – or hell, as later events were to prove. More imminent for Trivium, however, were gigs at the Ridglea Metal Festival in Texas, before hooking up with Chimara for a co-headline tour.

"It was awesome," Corey grinned later, "it was our second time out touring with them and they are such cool guys. It kicked ass!"[145]

When the news filtered through that Trivium would not only play at the annual Golden Gods awards ceremony for UK metal bible *Metal Hammer*, but were also nominated for 'Best International Newcomer', Corey could hardly hide his excitement.

"It's a real honour to be even nominated for an award like that," he enthused, "I'm not really sure but I believe it's quite a big deal. To win would be awesome as it would be our first award of that nature. We are really excited to be playing the awards show too with Anthrax, Shadows Fall and Nightwish. If we win there is going to be a lot of drinking. Even if we don't win there will be a lot of drinking."[146]

A lot of drinking? Surely not. A lot of drinking in the UK? Perish the thought. But the country that took the band into their hearts were about to be hit by a whirlwind of metal, the magnitude of which had not been seen since... well, You Know Who.

9

shredding it for the brits

The European leg of the Roadrage tour began on May 1 at Wolverhampton's Wulfrun Hall. Before the group played, there was the usual round of interviews to handle, one with 4Q Radio, an online video/radio site with a huge section dedicated to metal.

"Everyone's telling us that there's a lot of talk about us over here," offered Paolo, "these shows are gonna be the proof that people know our songs. That's awesome, considering that we had to go around the States three or four times before people really started getting into it. Out here, if people like a band they get really into it, which is how it should be."[147]

"I'm pumped for this tour," continued Corey, "cause we've been looking forward to coming out here and playing for a while. Plus, it's our first time on a bus, which makes it a lot easier to get rest and stuff. So, when we got here yesterday morning, we were actually able to get some sleep, which is something we've not really been able to do before."[148]

Europe was a more welcoming arena for the band; as their profile had soared, so had the haters – Trivium's own site had been spammed with abuse as the band became ubiquitous in the metal scene. In the UK, fans were happy to take the music at face value, glad that there was once more a group with great tunes and power – and a rock attitude to match. Not so in America.

"'Fuck you!' back. We don't give a shit what you think."

"Some other places we've played, some of the hardcore kids have been giving us some 'tough love'," continued Corey, "but they're getting into us now. We actually haven't played our home town for a while – so that's probably the place we've played least out of anywhere"[149]

"The thing is that when you don't show them that you care," continues the bassist, "and just laugh in their face, it's like a 'Fuck you!' back. We don't give a shit what you think."

There was also a backlash brewing, centred ridiculously on the way that Trivium dressed themselves, and their hair length (or lack thereof). "We dress the way we feel comfortable," said Paolo. "When we did our video, we dressed nice and shit. We're just trying to do our own thing."[150]

Their UK debut was superbly received, the excitement of the Brits palpable for the Roadrage lineup. At Wolverhampton, Trivium was the opening act, kicking things off with a bang. Webzine *Ultimate Metal* was massively impressed. "Bringing together into one explosive musical whole disparate influences from furious classic thrash, contemporary melodic death metal, metalcore-esque soaring choruses and a healthy dose of stadium-rock showmanship, the young Florida quartet start off the night in breathtaking style."[151]

UK metal 'zine *Satan's FishTank* – who had given the band their first ever UK cover in March – were also there. "Musically, these guys are spot on," wrote editor Rich Hatton, "not a fault in their set; from first song to last, they kick ass. These guys will be huge soon."[152]

Matt was enjoying himself: "We are having the time of our lives on our sweet tour bus, playing on the huge Euro stages, and rockin' out with some of the craziest motherfuckers out there."[153]

The craziness was catching to the point where the London gig on May 5 had to be upgraded from The Garage to the much bigger Mean Fiddler venue due to ticket demand. After a swift jaunt over to The Netherlands and Belgium to catch up with the European fans, Scotland was similarly bowled over by the band, Heafy goading the already-rapacious audience at Glasgow's King Tut's Wah Wah Hut into a melée of limbs and screams, a rash of circle-moshing, walls of death and sending the whole venue into a frenzy of electric madness. Encores on the tour included 'Master Of Puppets' and Iron Maiden's classic cut from the 1983 *Piece Of Mind* album, 'The Trooper'. If there were any doubt as to where the roots of Trivium's approach lay, they were assuaged thereby.

The tour was massive; crowds in the UK were battered from pillar to post by the sheer energy and quality in front of them – the British leg of proceedings ended at Brighton on May 18, a day after *Kerrang! TV* began showing the video to 'Pull Harder On The Strings Of Your Martyr'.

It had been a triumph, and as the tour rumbled into the European mainland, the pace flagged for not a second. Paolo Gregoletto had a chance to hook up with his Italian heritage on May 28, Trivium ripping it up at Milan's Transalvania club – a date, like many on the tour, that was being filmed with a view to putting together a performance-based video for 'A Gunshot To The Head Of Trepidation'. Initially, Rage Resteghini was mooted to produce a narrative-based piece of film for the track, but as it turned out, both Resteghini and Trivium's already-bulging schedules didn't allow for such a hook-up.

Roadrunner had done a great job in promoting the Roadrage part of the 25th anniversary celebrations, but they also had an absolute bang-on gem of an idea up their sleeves, as they unveiled to the world on May 30.

The label had been reissuing classic albums – one for each year of their existence – but how best to bring together the old and the new, the people that shared an attitude and a vision, those who shared a love for the gnarly and a yearning for the grime-clad wrathful riffs that had been so influential over the last twenty five years?

Brainwave. Get musicians from all the bands on the roster together and write some new music to be released on an album. Supergroups amongst supergroups. What better to call such an LP than *Roadrunner United: The All-Star Sessions*?

Of course, in order to make some sort of sense from the vast amount of talent available, four team captains were selected to pick people with whom to work. So it was that Slipknot's Joey Jordison, Dino Canizares of Fear Factory and Rob Flynn from Machine Head were chosen – as was one Matt Heafy, the nineteen-year-old upstart whose group were rapidly being seen to have the potential to join the aforementioned bands as timeless heavyweights of metal.

"All four musicians will not only play on the songs they've written, but will assemble a team of artists to record the tracks," wrote MTV.com, "in order to cover as wide a spectrum as possible, no musician will play for more than one writer/producer and each song will feature a different vocalist. The project is being overseen by longtime Roadrunner A&R man Monte Conner. Mixing duties will be handled by legendary hard rock producer Colin Richardson."[154]

"And I said, 'Fuck, yeah. Fuuuuck, yeah!'"

For Heafy's part, the wheel had turned full circle; Slipknot's typesetter-confusing opus, '(sic)', having been the first ever song that Trivium had played in the live arena, "because it was a great opener."

All the bands on the Roadrunner roster would provide musicians for the team captains to select for their recording sessions. One whole buncha metal talent!

"Literally they gave me a huge check list with names [to choose from]," Matt continued, "and I could pick whoever I wanted to.[155] [Monte Conner] said, 'do you want to write a song for King Diamond?' And I said, 'Fuck, yeah. Fuuuuck, yeah!'"[156]

Trivium's last appearance on the European Road Rage tour was on June 9, at Amsterdam's Melkweg (Milky Way) venue – a show that was webcast on fabchannel.com – presumably on computers that had survived the insane paranoia of the millennium bug some five years previously. The Roadrage tour actually culminated 4 REAL the following day in Nancy, France – but the band had to pull out of the climactic date in order to travel back to the UK for a rescheduled appearance at the Download festival.

Download, formerly known as Monsters Of Rock, is held in Donington Park, home to the Grand Prix racetrack, and can be considered *the* major rock festival in Europe; Trivium had slammed it at two German shindigs – Rock Am Ring, and Nuremburg's Rock Im Park – but, let's make no mistake here, playing Download was and is a definitive sign that a band have arrived on the scene. For Trivium's part, they had long been booked to play the Napster New Bands stage on Sunday 12, a great showcase for their talents. But between having been pencilled in as one of many promising, upcoming acts and the subsequent massive momentum that the band was gathering around them, it had very quickly become clear that Trivium were an act that required a slightly bigger arena.

The news came through. Trivium were now scheduled to open Saturday's lineup at the festival. Saturday was 'Ozzfest day' at Download; since the band had been selected for that shebang the goalposts had changed somewhat.

"We can't wait – we're so excited," enthused Heafy. "The support from everyone in the UK has been fantastic and to get upgraded to the Main Stage at the legendary Donington is just amazing. We hope everyone has as much fun as we plan to!"[157]

Upgraded to play on the main stage, sure, but at eleven o' clock? That's eleven o'clock in the MORNING? Eleven o'clock on a SATURDAY MORNING? Eleven o'clock on a SATURDAY MORNING, the Saturday morning after the Friday night post-first-night parties, during which festival-goers traditionally, and spectacularly, drink themselves into ditches and spend the night trying to fiddle with the squidgy, unctuous contents of each other's britches?

There'd be not a single sane rocker getting up at eleven o'clock the morning after the rampant night before, surely…

128

10

Insanity

Thirty thousand people turned up.

Download is clearly not the place for sanity. That's considerably more than the previous night's headline act, Feeder, could pull. And considerably more than 90% of the bands pulled all weekend.

Kerrang! put it thus: "11am might seem a bit early to witness the future of metal, but judging by the vast crowd that's turned up for Trivium (KKKKK) the Florida foursome's ascent to legendary status is already underway. From the acoustic intro to 'End Of Everything' to breathtaking set-closer 'Pull Harder On The Strings Of Your Martyr', the devotion on display is – for such a new band – unprecedented. Frontman Matt Heafy looks like a young James Hetfield, utterly assured of his own impending stardom. At one point there's six circle-pits going off at once as riffs rain down like lava. What a spectacle. What a start to the day. What an awesome fucking band."[158] It was, arguably, Trivium's greatest gig to date and unquestionably their most important. After this set, everything changed for them *forever*.

That awesome band, borne on increasingly glorious wings, flashed down to London Astoria on June 13 to perform at the influential *Metal Hammer* Golden Gods Awards. It was a suitably raucous night, as a thousand bands, journalists and lucky competition winners saw Lemmy pick up the 'Golden God' award, Roadrunner 'Best Label', and Lostprophets snagging 'Best UK Band' (being roundly booed by certain sections of the audience when they wandered up to accept the award). In the event, Trivium was pipped by Nightwish to 'Best International Newcomer'. No matter: the celebrations went on long into the night regardless.

Clocking up the air miles once more, Trivium returned to the US for some R&R before a June 21 shooting session – complete with a baying crowd of invited fans – to complete the performance-based video for 'A Gunshot To The Head Of Trepidation'.

July began in the greatest way possible, the band scoring the cover feature for *Kerrang!* magazine. "Saturday June 11, 2005 will be remembered as the day the UK fell in love with Trivium," begun the piece, "at a stroke, their ecstatically received Download festival performance – at which a 30,000-strong crowd went collectively apeshit at 11am – transformed Trivium from up-and-coming newbies into genuine global contenders. The band's cutting-edge take on classic thrash, combined with frontman Matt Heafy's startling, stadium-size star quality, has made Trivium *the* name to drop in metal circles – as demonstrated by the current, lightning-fast proliferation of Trivium T-shirts and hoodies."

The band reaffirmed their intent to take Trivium to the status of Metallica, shared tour stories, and generally roared with cast-iron self belief. And, of course, there's offstage shenanigans to which to allude. "We're very fucking rock 'n' roll," cackled Matt, "sex 'n' drugs, man, we're turning into the next Mötley Crüe!"[159]

"Ozzy has everything to do with saving Metal"

There would be plenty of opportunities to prove this as the band joined Ozzfest on July 15 with a gig in the Tweeter Centre in Mansfield, Massachusets. The concept – a travelling metal festival – fills a hole in the US that is comparable to the impact of Download and Rock Am Ring in Europe, and it was celebrating its 10th anniversary in 2005.

"Ozzy has everything to do with saving Metal," says Matt Wagner, "it's the only major tour that really brought people out of the woodwork. So we have a whole new generation of metalheads, plus the commercialisation of it – Cradle Of Filth T-shirts in the malls; it's become fashionable for metal to be cool again. A lot of these kids are coming out of high school, turning into adults, supporting the scene, coming to the shows."

To say Ozzfest is high-profile is something of an understatement. Trivium's participation was a massive boost to their profile. And the initial gigs were exceptionally well-received.

Iron Maiden stole the show most nights,[160] while Trivium, for their part, concentrated on hammering out their nascent classics on the second stage; happy to be on the tour, they spent their time drinking in the atmosphere, the banter, and no doubt the Jägermeister.[161] They were, by now, a huge draw in the UK – the news coming through that the tickets for their forthcoming *Kerrang! Most Wanted* gig on August 24 had sold out in a mere two hours. As August rolled on, the band continued to pick up fans throughout America. With the news that they'd been nominated in two categories in the *Kerrang!* awards: 'Best International Newcomer' and for 'Best Album' for *Ascendancy* as well as appearing on TV's *Fuse* Ozzfest special, and coming second in *Yahoo! Music*'s 'Dig It Or Diss It' online vote for best video,[162] all was groovy in Trivium-land.

"I wouldn't dare throw anything at Maiden, not even money."

In Ozzfest-land, however, things were becoming a little more fractious. Relationships between Iron Maiden and the Ozzy camp came to an inevitable head on August 20, when the venerable Sharon Osbourne clashed with Maiden singer, Bruce Dickinson. On tour, Dickinson had been consistently commenting to the crowd about how he didn't need a reality TV show to give him credibility; provocative words that were taken to directly relate to the hit MTV programme, *The Osbournes* – a fly-on-the-wall documentary tracing the day-to-day ups and downs of Prince Of Darkness Ozzy and his dysfunctional family.

Following the Maiden singer's comments, eggs and other debris were thrown at his band, the PA was cut during songs and the explosion happened. Maiden left the tour to be replaced by Velvet Revolver. It was an astonishing clash of titans, with both sides blaming the other for allowing such a wedge to be driven between the show's ethos and the participants. Whilst the media had a field day concerning the blow-up between metal legends, the rest of the line-up found themselves caught in the crossfire.

Travis, however, hadn't seen the incident, telling *Satan's FishTank* that he "was drinking. Paolo witnessed it all, and he came back to the bus and was going off about it. But I was just stood outside drinking beer, he came back and said some shit went down. I just thought, 'Holy fuck.'"[163]

The next show that Trivium played on the tour – in Albuquerque – saw the band making their stand. They all wore Maiden T-shirts, aligning themselves with the UK veterans.

"All the bands and all the crews knew what we were trying to say," Heafy told *Metal Hammer*, "there were gangs of people from the bands on the second stage trying to recruit people to throw eggs at Maiden. Man, I wouldn't dare throw anything at Maiden, not even money. I watched them from right at the front at one show and I did everything, every gesture that Bruce asked of the crowd. I was too afraid not to."[164]

On August 24, during a concert at London's tiny Barfly venue, the band were joined onstage by Rob Flynn of Machine Head – with whom Matt had been collaborating on the 'Roadrunner All-Stars' sessions. Flynn helped the band hammer through a series of classic covers including Sepultura's 'Roots' in a low-profile gig scheduled before the *Kerrang!* awards show the next day.

Trivium's love affair with the UK was becoming more passionate by the day. And when the band picked up the award for 'Best International Newcomer', it was a moment to savour.

"It was our first time at the awards which was amazing in itself," said Travis, "but sitting at our table and hearing them call out name was just a 'Holy shit' moment. It was really awesome; we were walking up to the stage and the only thing I could think of to say was 'Fuck yeah!'"

"We were at our table," continued the drummer, "and Dave Grohl walks over, pats us on our shoulder and says, 'I've just got your new album – it's fucking excellent.' Dave Grohl is incredible to me, he's just an amazing musician."[165]

Respected journalist Mark Sutherland (ex-Music News Editor at BBC's flagship digital radio station, 6Music and, at the time of this interview, London Bureau Chief for *Billboard*), remembers interviewing the band at the awards. "They were all wearing Iron Maiden T-shirts, and were all very vocal about [what happened at Ozzfest]," comments Sutherland. "I think most of the other young bands on that Ozzfest bill wouldn't have had the bottle to do that. It was interesting, you'd think that everyone would side with the Osbournes – cause that's where the power lies – but Trivium were very vocal in their support of Iron Maiden. Which makes sense, cause in many ways they're an homage to Iron Maiden, and old school metal in general."

The old-school bent of 'Pull Harder…' was released as part of the soundtrack to the movie, *The Cave*, on August 26 – the band are in great company on the album, with tracks also coming from the likes of Mastodon, It Dies Today, Shadows Fall and Nightwish. The movie may be a run-of-the-mill Creature Feature, an unremarkable horror tale of divers and monsters, but the soundtrack is a snapshot of some of the best names in metal of the time.

It was time to return to the UK, a country that had treated the band with such esteem. Trivium smashed back to a rather shellshocked Blighty still reeling from terrorist bombings on the London Underground system on 7/7, 2005. But it was also a country ready to stand up, unmoved, and get on with life: a country with the fortitude that allowed its inhabitants to get out there and have some fun and damn those who would seek to break their spirit.

The 'Ascendancy' tour continued throughout that month on the back of the news that – thanks to album sales having increased seven weeks in a row – *Ascendancy* was Roadrunner's best-selling debut since Slipknot in 1999. As ever, the gigs – also featuring All That Remains and It Dies Today – were blinding. All dates were sold out, and the response from the crowd was consistently extraordinary.

"At the moment in the UK I think the reason we're pretty popular is that I don't think there are many bands that want to go out their way to make their show something memorable," suggested the bassist, "I was there when Trivium played to six, seven hundred kids, and put on a full show, had the full lights, made it seem like it was an arena, but made it like really personal. That was the whole thing with this tour – to keep it really intimate."[166]

"We dressed up and did some stupid shit."

The tour featured a few 'rest days'. Trivium, however, do not know the meaning of the word: with the bit between their teeth, dates were booked for a 'tribute band' under the rather transparently obvious name, Ember And The Infernos. Donning silly wigs, crazy 'taches and all manner of rawwwk stagewear, 'The Infernos' offered a set of classic metal covers and – of course – Trivium songs at shows in London, Dublin, Cardiff and Birmingham. It was a typically playful statement from the band; their profile had never been higher as credible musicians, and they may have been aggressively up-front about their intentions to become a massive band, but it sure as hell wasn't gonna stop them having some fun!

"The shows were amazing," laughed Matt, "we dressed up and did some stupid shit, it was really fun. We played a bunch of ridiculous covers like Blink-182, Nirvana, Metallica and Rammstein, lots of silly shit."[167]

Immediately following the UK gigs, Trivium headed into Europe for a series of dates with Dark Tranquility and Arch Enemy – travelling from France to Belgium, Germany and the Netherlands before wowing Scandinavian audiences in Norway, Sweden and Denmark. Some mileage to cover in a little over two weeks!

The autumn of 2005 saw the release schedule also chockablock; first off, Roadrunner released a special edition version of *Ascendancy* to coincide with the tour; *Ember To Inferno* was re-released again by Lifeforce (charting at Number 20 in the UK Independent Album Charts, and Number 22 in the UK Rock & Metal Chart); the band's 'Pull Harder...' was on the soundtrack of the PS2 game *Infected*; and – perhaps most intriguingly – the long-anticipated *Roadrunner United* CD hit the shelves, with an accompanying DVD complete with behind the scenes interviews with team captains and in-studio footage. These were unique moments in time never to be repeated, but luckily also captured for posterity.

Heafy's involvement as a captain meant he wrote and played guitar on four tracks: 'In The Fire', featuring King Diamond, Mike D'Antonio of Killswitch Engage, Ill Niño's Dave Chivarri and one Corey Beaulieu; 'Dawn Of A Golden Age', the musicians being Justin Hagberg (3 Inches Of Blood), ex-Cynic man Sean Malone on bass, Suffocation drummer Mike Smith and vocalist Dani Filth; 'Blood And Flames', a track boasting Killswitch Engage bassist Mike D'Antonio, Josh Silver of Type O Negative, Stone Sour guitarist Josh Rand, with Jesse Leach, late of Killswitch Engage, on vocals; and 'I Don't Wanna Be (A Superhero)' where the impressive musicians involved were ex-Misfits vocalist Michale Graves, plus a backing of D'Antonio, Hagberg and Chivarri.

Matt also sang on the Dino Canizares-penned 'The End', for which a video was shot – the reprobates responsible for the music this time being Nadja Peulen of Coal Chamber, Roy Mayroga – ex-Soulfly, Logan Mader, late of Machine Head, and Front Line Assembly's Rhys Fulber. It was premiered on Fuse TV on October 12.

Albeit a record that was thrown together round the schedules of the magnificent musicians involved, it is also a project that speaks volumes of the talent of the people involved in the process and their collective love for the label and its metal output. It's probably fair to say that we'll never see the likes of it again – until the fiftieth anniversary, at least.

The end of October brought an emotional return to the land of the singer's birth; five shows were scheduled in Japan, somewhere Matt Heafy had been longing to visit throughout all of those years rehearsing in his bedroom, those long days bashing away in dank rehearsal studios preparing for a gig at DIY or FBI – despite the moments of doubt and distress caused by the shedding of band members and reshuffling Team Trivium, it was all coming full circle.

The five shows ranged between seven hundred and two thousand in capacity, and though Trivium was the relatively unknown act in comparison to Arch Enemy, it was a tour full of spark and energy. Yuka Hirose, who runs the first ever Japanese Trivium website, caught them on tour.

"They hadn't headlined in Japan before," muses Hirose, "Tokyo was the most packed show, because there were more American fans, army people. The other dates weren't packed, even though Arch Enemy was playing. Metal and hardcore are not really big in Japan so it is really hard to get noticed. There's never much circle pit action or moshing going around in Japanese gigs."

"Most of the Arch Enemy fans didn't know who they were, or what kind of music they play. But when Trivium started, most of the fans were quite impressed and after the show I think most of the Arch Enemy fans liked it." Heafy took every opportunity to catch up with his heritage. "Matt tried to speak in Japanese," continues Yuka. "They played in Hiroshima, which is a minor city, but it is really near where Matt was born so it was great to go to there, and I heard that Matt met with his grandparents."[168]

What a summer and autumn it had been: Trivium were on top of the world as they set out for their latest tour of the US, this time alongside Children Of Bodom. "It's going to be amazing," said Matt. "We're huge fans of Children of Bodom and if the crowds have been reacting anything like we're used to from the UK and Europe then it's going to be a knockdown, drag out good time."[169]

Was it?

II

Brickbats and Bouncebacks

The gigs were to take in venues across Canada and the States, virtually a month's worth of live work starting on November 9. Given the explosion of interest from the UK, Trivium's quest to get their name out to a larger audience throughout America was paramount. The Finnish metallers provided an audience leaning more toward the classically symphonic/dark black and death metal side of matters. The other band on the bill, Stockholm's Amon Amarth, slotted into the Viking thematic with a dark power, something that Trivium had a great affinity with, as Matt's dalliance with Mindscar back in the early days of the century had shown – and there's also the little matter of the hefty Capharnaum to consider. He also had an on-paper death/black metal band project buzzing around his bonce, though for the time being any such ventures had little chance of sliding into Trivium's busting schedule. It was felt that Trivium would pick up fans from the relative veterans' audience, whilst bringing in a new breed of scoundrels to the equation.[170]

Unfortunately, some sections of the hardcore-black-death audience were unhappy with the Floridians' growing status and musical approach, and voiced their displeasure accordingly. "They held up pretty well in the face of a few scornful death metal fans," wrote a reviewer, "their scream-sing-scream-sing formula mixing melodic sing-along choruses with thrashy verses and huge breakdowns had a particularly decent effect on the younger crowd."[171]

Trivium just got on with it: heckling in itself is a measure of their success. Corey also became an old man during this tour, turning the grand old age of 22 at the Vancouver date. Not a bad way to celebrate a birthday! And as usual, Trivium rose above everything to deliver wicked, roof-shaking gigs with a band that had been one of Heafy's favourites for some years. The grumblings from sections of the crowd, however, culminated in some rather un-Christian bottle-throwing and expletive-filled vitrol directed at Trivium at San Fransisco's Slim's venue the very next night.

Not that Bodom bassist Henkka Seppälä was overly worried about their tour mates' credentials. "Amon Amarth and Trivium are great to tour with," he said, "they ensure that we have packed venues every night. We get along with the Swedes very well, as so with Trivium dudes. Couple of them have ended up getting wasted and sleeping on our bus too!!!"[172]

Ah, the international language of fuckedness. Second only to football in its ability to reach across nations.[173]

As November drew to a close, Trivium were once more subjects of a *Yahoo!* online poll – this time coming up trumps in that site's 'Who's Next' vote, accumulating 37% and winning the opportunity to perform two tracks from the album and record an interview which was broadcast in December. The win was described by Heafy as "amazing, and humbling".

The Bodom tour reached Washington, DC on December 8, 2005. This was a date which had taken on an added sadness – it was the first anniversary of the murder onstage of Pantera guitarist Darrel Lance Abbot Darrell – known and loved by many as 'Dimebag'. Dimebag, along with three others, had been shot onstage at a concert in Columbus, Ohio by a frenzied Nathan Gale. It was an horrendous incident that had sent shockwaves throughout not only the metal community, but fans of music worldwide.

By way of a tribute, Trivium played 'Domination' and part of 'Walk' to show their respect to a man who'd inspired them all so much. Dimebag's long-time girlfriend Rita Haney brought them two guitars that Dime had played on the last Pantera tour, for the show: a Rebel/Confederate Washburn and a diamond-plated, 'Reinventing The Steel' written-up-the-fretboard Washburn. The band later thanked her on their website, where a video of the band's performance of 'Domination' was later posted for downloading.

Total Guitar magazine named Trivium its first ever 'Band Of The Year', and the group also found themselves cover stars of *Decibel* in the US. News came through also that the unreleased track, 'Washing Away Me In The Tides' was on the soundtrack to the computer game 'Underworld: Evolution' – the album, also featuring Alkaline Trio, Aiden and Slipknot, was subsequently released on Lifeforce on Jan 10, 2006.

Following the Bodom tour, and unable to actually sit down for more than six seconds without having to create something, the band hooked up with Rage Resteghini to shoot the final video from 'Ascendancy' – this time the track in question was 'Dying In Your Arms'.

"It was to be a take on Phantom Of The Opera," explains Rage, "me and my team drove all the way to Philadelphia a few days before with all kinds of period piece costumes and the masks which we had created. It was a massive production. I spent time doing a storyboard, and renting a killer location. It came out amazing. I mean, the video, for the budget we had to work with, it was their third video off the record, and everybody loved it." Ultimately, however, the final released promo was a montage of live pieces.

"Domination over everything else is the ultimate goal."

December 15 was a legendary day, with the live Roadrunner United show bringing together the massed ranks of people involved in the project. The core backing band for the show, at New York's Nokia Theatre, featured Joey Jordison on drums, Dino Canizares on guitar, Machine Head's Adam Duce on bass and Andrea Kisser shredding away on the axe. It was a party to end all parties; Heafy and Rob Flynn duetting on 'Pull Harder' before all retired for a raucous knees-up.

Trivium had for some time been messing with riffs for potential new tracks, and took the opportunity of fine-tuning and rehearsing original material that had been written on the road over the previous eight months or thereabouts. It was time to start thinking seriously about the recordings for a new album to take advantage of the fact that, despite having been out since March, *Ascendancy* was still selling faster than ever, to the tune of 3,000 copies a week. It had also gone silver in the UK during December, having sold in excess of 60,000 units.

Although the Ozzfest tour had been more eventful than anyone could have realised, Trivium nevertheless were part of the 10th Anniversary DVD, contributing their now-legendary Download performance of 'A Gunshot To The Head Of Trepidation' to the release. *Ascendancy* had been named 'Album Of The Year' by readers of *Kerrang!*, *Rock Sound* and UK extreme metal magazine *Terroriser*, the new sessions had a huge amount to live up to, for sure, cause 2005 was a memorable year in anyone's money.

The concept for the new long-player was, as usual, pretty fully formed already. Keeping in the now-established tradition of having album titles and concepts that sat neatly with the band's career – as well as a good dollop of classic heavy metal connotations, the new album was to be called *The Crusade*. "It's not based on the actual Crusades," explained Corey, "every Trivium album has been representative of where the band has been at the time. 'Ember To Inferno' meant we were going from a little spark to something special, 'Ascendancy' is the gradual rise, living out the dream of having a higher power or domination of everything else. And 'The Crusade' is what we have been doing; crusading over the fucking planet for the last year and a half!"

"Domination over everything else is the ultimate goal," agreed Matt, "when we become the biggest band in the world! But I think the biggest point of ascendancy will be after the crusades!"[174]

Mocking the tag of metalcore, Trivium revealed a much wider sphere of influence for this new record: "We're listening to a lot of Dream Theater and stuff like that," he concluded. "We're trying to put the guitar playing on a higher level and create a more epic kind of sound. Some songs will be typically Trivium – heavy rocking groove stuff – but some will be more on the technical, progressive side. It will still be easy for someone to listen to because of the melody. Another idea was changing the vocal style. Less of the brutal, screaming metalcore thing, more of a sort of James Hetfield-esque thing like on *...And Justice For All*. We have some ideas we want to add to the new record instead of coming out with *Ascendancy 2*. It really has to be something on its own."[175]

As 2005 turned into 2006, Travis and Corey travelled to Texas to see in the New Year in style, with a typically wild piece of partying. Hooking up with Rita Haney, the motley bunch headed out for some live music and, uh, a few shandies.

"Did we have a fuckin' blast!" laughed Corey, "we went to see Vinnie Paul's cover band Gasoline on New Year's night, and I got to play 'Cowboys From Hell' with Vinnie and Rex – that was an unreal time! I was hammered too which made it even more of a badass time."

"After that we had a fireworks party back at the Dimes' pad and I burnt my hand; we set the lawn on fire, the cops came; [we] chased people around the house with roman candles, threw fireworks in Brent Young's room and accidentally set the blanket on fire, drank 5 bottles of Jäger, 4 bottles of Seagram, 7 bottles of Crown and 2-3 cases of beer - and we got the whole thing on video tape! Stay tuned for the Trivium DVD to catch that shit – haha."[176]

2006 continued in the same full-on gigging vein, with the band out on the road with In Flames, Devildriver and Zao for much of January and February. They would have to cope, however, without their drum tech Mike Rafferty, who'd been headhunted by the band Demiricious to pick up the sticks and kick some shit behind the kit for a change. It seemed that the Trivium camp was providing musicians and inspiration all over the place (their road crew during 2004-5 also included the 'legendary' Brian Mock, one-time band mate of Richie Brown in Mindscar). The gigs were sold out, electric and fizzing, putting memories of the darker days of crowd abuse and bad vibes firmly in the past. When the band reached Orlando's House Of Blues for their first appearance since late 2004, the joint was absolutely rockin'.

"Did we have a fuckin' blast!"

"Orlando boys Trivium owned the stage like it was their own," a reviewer mused, "mixing metalcore with a more progressive sound, Trivium has steadily been inching its way to stardom since the band's inception in 2000. Judging by the way the floor almost caves in under the weight of stomping boots, these guys may have just arrived on stardom's doorstep. As if their own music hadn't already turned on the crowd, their tribute to Pantera ('this one's for Dimebag Darrell') nailed it home."[177]

An instore appearance in San Fransisco had seen the band mobbed and the shop groaning under the weight of Trivium fans – little wonder given that the group had recently won 'Best Newcomer' and 'Best Album' in *Metal Hammer*'s readers' poll. Heafy scored fifth in the 'Man Of The Year' category (it was won by Bruce Dickinson).

February began with Trivium scoring front covers of both *Metal Hammer* and *Kerrang!*, and amongst the chat about the forthcoming album, there was also a new and rather surprising admission: the year and a half of rock-star sex, sex and rock 'n' roll was beginning to take its toll. Gone, perhaps, were the wild days of groupies and JDs. With the band headlining their 'The Crusade: Ascend

Above The Ashes' UK tour alongside God Forbid and Bloodsimple (it was already near as damnit sold out), and the video for 'Dying In Your Arms' debuting on most of the major channels (it was the most played video on *Kerrang! TV* in the first week in March), were the late and licentious nights actually beginning to catch up with the band?

"I didn't want to get to the point where I hated myself."

"I don't do that anymore," Heafy explained to *Metal Hammer* in a typically frank interview, "I didn't want to become one of *those* people. I didn't want to get to the point where I hated myself. I didn't want to get to the point where I was just using people, using women, just because they were there and they were available to me. It's very easy to do. You're on a tour bus, you're bored; there's a woman there who's willing to fuck you and you fuck her because you can. But there's an emptiness to it that you cannot escape. There's no connection there other than a physical one. And the whole experience drains you. It drains you emotionally, and it drains you mentally. And if you carry on doing it, it *will* take a toll."

"And the same with drink. I didn't want to get loaded every night, but I was. I was drinking way too much. I was never big into drugs, but I would take coke and I hate myself for that. I've decided to cut back on the drink because I've taken the time to remind myself why I'm doing this. And the reason is because of the music we create."[178]

With stakes getting ever-higher, it's no surprise that Heafy stepped back from the wrecking to concentrate on the shredding. The spring of 2006 culminated in interviews on BBC 6Music for the band on Bruce Dickinson's radio show, a session at the legendary Maida

Vale studios for BBC Radio One,[179] and more high-profile releases, including a special edition of *Ascendancy* with all four videos on its DVD, and 'Washing Away Me In The Tides' added to the track-listing of the CD proper.

Kerrang Remastered was a project instigated by that magazine to celebrate the 20th Anniversary of the release of *Master Of Puppets*. A host of bands were invited to contribute a cover version of one of that album's tracks to the CD – given away free with issue 1102 – and Trivium, being majorly inspired by Metallica, were bolt-ons for inclusion, with their version of the title track suitably shredding.

"I don't want to sound like a cocky asshole, but I wasn't worried about choosing this song at all," said Matt, "Hetfield used to hit the high notes pretty fucking high back in the day, so for me, the most fun was recording the vocals. I hope that when Metallica hear it they realise that they're the main reason why we're here today. If they do like it, it'll be such a triumph for us!"[180]

On April 11, Roadrunner released *Headbangers Ball: The Revenge* – a double disc audio compilation of MTV2's flagship show. Trivium contributed 'A Gunshot To The Head Of Trepidation' to the compilation. 'Ember And The Infernos' had accompanied Trivium to the UK as ever, and the 'tribute' band wowed audiences suitably at London's Islington Academy; the 'real' Trivium, meanwhile, were making their fans' dreams come true by running a competition for one of them to join the band onstage to play during their set – Scott Bennett won, and had the experience of a lifetime in front of a packed Birmingham Academy on March 9. The group's connection with the fans was as strong as ever, and when the doors were mistakenly opened during a soundcheck whilst the band rehearsed at Bradford's Rio venue, the response from the band was typical. They asked the fans onstage to join them for some cover versions of bands such as Metallica, Iron Maiden and, of course, their own stuff. "Everyone seemed to enjoy it, I know we did! It was incredible!" said Matt. "Afterward we hung out for about an hour and a half and chilled."[181]

Trivium were booked for most of the major European festivals by this point, including a triumphant return to Download – much higher up the bill this time, of course, on June 10 where the headliners were… You Know Who… the might of Metallica. On April 15, Trivium were also nominated in an unprecedented four categories for *Metal Hammer*'s annual Golden Gods Awards: 'Best Live Band', 'Best International Band', 'Best Shredder' and 'Best Drummer' (Roadrunner were up for a gong as 'Best Label') The group spent late April in Audiohammer with Suecof, beginning to lay down tracks for 'The Crusade'. This is what being in a band is *really* about.

Things couldn't get any better, surely.

12

maiden Heaven

Better? Ha! Try this for size.

It was announced that Trivium were to be Iron Maiden's support on the European dates of their world tour in the autumn and winter of 2006.

"Trivium is extremely honoured to be given the opportunity to tour with the legendary Iron Maiden," an excited Heafy said, "arguably the greatest metal band of all time. Maiden has influenced many bands, including Trivium, with their music – a mix of sheer power and melody, and also with their amazing stage productions. A few words to express our band's mutual reaction: 'Holy fuck, we're touring with Iron Maiden!!!!'"[182]

"Iron Maiden are one of my favourite bands ever! The first time I heard Maiden was when I was 13: the first song I heard was 'The Trooper', which I'd recommend to anyone getting into Maiden for the first time," Matt told legendary rock journo, Joel McIver: "We play that song a lot live. Then I got into the *Seventh Son Of A Seventh Son* album, which I love – every single track on it is a classic! At that time everything else was really simple, and Maiden's songs were really hard to play – way more technical than anything else at the time. One thing that you'll hear in the metal and metalcore scenes right now is that everybody's into dual harmonised guitar lines. Whether the musicians realise it or not, that all goes directly back to Maiden. They weren't the first band to do it, but without them nobody would be doing that shit in a metal band with that degree of prominence."

"The thing that makes Iron Maiden so special," he continued, "is that they never went out of their way to overhaul their sound, like a lot of big bands do. They realised what works for them and always stayed true to what they are. They are truly individual. In this business it should be about doing what the artist truly wants to do – and Maiden have always done exactly what they wanted. We try to do the same as Maiden – to play the style of metal we want to play, regardless of what everyone else is doing."

"The thing that makes Iron Maiden's songs stand out after so many years is simple – it's because they're so good. They don't sound like anybody else: as soon as you hear that bass line you know it's Steve Harris. Their songs are full of epic sounds: you've got different vocal and guitar melodies going on at the same time, which are just incredible. Every instrumentalist in the band adds something unique."

Perhaps as incredible is the fact that Corey had once jammed with Maiden drummer Nicko McBrain, prior to the guitarist joining Trivium. "He lives in Boca Raton, which is about 10 minutes from where I live," said Beaulieu. "There was this festival and I was playing there with my band and we ended up jamming with him. We did 'Aces High' and 'The Wickerman'. That was really amazing."[183]

Amazing, indeed.

"It's a straight out thrash metal album."

With tails up, Trivium's sessions for *The Crusade* began in earnest. It's an LP that – perhaps unsurprisingly – takes the inherent Trivium blueprint, develops it, and comes out with a collection of songs that are not only more coherent than before, but display the band's musical experience and influence in prismatic 3D.

"It's a straight out thrash metal album", Corey said. "We tried to make sure, on the new record, that when people hear it, they can tell the difference, because the last record got compared to metalcore and crap like that."

Seven strings, multiple tempos and time signatures, Pantera-esque vocals, and even more polished musicality, it was impressive stuff. "You can still be heavy and brutal, but now you'll hear what the person's saying instead of just being super-heavy. So we wanted to change that because every band fucking screams and shit nowadays, so we wanted to be different. Matt's got a singing style that he doesn't really use – and didn't use on the last record – but it sounds really cool and it's more unique to him."[184] It was more diverse too, drawing in snatches of Skid Row, Rammstein, Mötley Crüe, Dio and Dokken, even 'The Legacy'-era Testament.[185/186]

Trivium recorded throughout May and June, before the multitracks were sent over to the UK once more for fairy dust-sprinkling from another of their heroes; this time Colin Richardson was to mix the album. Richardson's work with the likes of Slipknot, Fear Factory and Machine Head made him the perfect choice.

"You have a vision of where you want to take it," explained the producer to the author, "and it's just a matter of trying ideas out to accomplish this. Sonically I'm not sure it's different [from *Ascendancy*] but riff-wise it's more of a rock record, and also there is no screaming anymore."

"They sounded great when I saw them live, and hopefully the mix has the same power," he concludes, "I didn't have a specific approach to individual tracks, just tried to make everything as big, punchy as possible." He succeeded: the results found favour with none other than Kirk Hammett, to whom Matt had sent one of the earliest post-production mixes.

"It's made me proud how far they've come since then."

Download 2006 was affirmation that Trivium were now at the upper strata of metal. Not only did the band play one of the highest slots on the bill on June 10, they also shared a stage with the band that had inspired them to pick up their guitars in the first place. If there is a moment of utter triumph and validation, it is the moment that the dreams converged with the reality. When headliners Metallica came back to encore with a cover of The Misfits' 'Die, Die My Darling', the guys from Trivium stepped onstage to perform with them. It got better: on June 12 *Metal Hammer* awarded Trivium 'Best Drummer', 'Best Live Band' and crowned Matt Heafy as its 2006 'Golden God', with Roadrunner picking up 'Best Label'. The band's schedule throughout the rest of the year was already full of touring action – the festivals of the summer would be immediately followed by the Sounds Of The Underground tour alongside the likes of In Flames, As I Lay Dying, Cannibal Corpse and Gwar, and the year would end in the best possible way with those incredible Maiden dates.

It was the culmination of six years of hard work and hard knocks, hard drinking and harsh hours driving thousands of miles in clapped out vans. The dedication to the cause had never wavered, even through the dark days of unstable line-ups, nor had Trivium lost heart under the provocation of other bands' fans and their vocal – and occasionally physical – abuse. This was not only a band, but now, firmly, a lifestyle – and the age of its members means that there is yet more to come.

"They're really young, they could probably go anywhere with it," muses Hardcore George Moore, "which is kinda scary. Cause they're so big, and if they do eventually want to branch out and experiment and do different things, then they're gonna catch fuckin' flak for it. And that's not gonna be cool for them, cause they're already this huge metal band with this sound, and people are so devoted to how it is now."

Matt Wagner, so instrumental in the band's early career, beams at the success of the group since the early days. "It's made me proud how far they've come since then," he says. "My God! They're opening for Iron Maiden. I would cut off one of my testicles in a heartbeat to open for Iron Maiden on a stadium tour. I mean, come on! To have that opportunity is just incredible. You know, when they come into town I feel like one of the parents. I've sat up in the balcony of the House Of Blues with Matt's dad, and Paolo's mom, and Travis' dad, and I felt like I was watching my kids onstage. I'm very proud of them."

"But Matt always had a maturity about him," he concludes, "even being nineteen years old and being a local star, he was always a very humble guy. He never came across as a pompous smartass. He's always been very polite, very grounded. He never had any ambitions or expectations beyond what was in front of him at the time – they were all just happy to just be onstage, playing and having fun with their friends. That's what it's all about. I say that if you're in it for any other reason then you're in music for the wrong reasons anyway. Cause there's no money in it – unless you get lucky!"

"It is like being married to three other people."

"Realistically, the life expectancy of a band these days is much shorter than it was in, say, the 80s – when you could put out an album a year, or every two years, and retain that fan base as new trends and fashions came through. So for a band like Trivium to come in and basically reintroduce the guitar solo to a whole new generation of people – it's unimaginable – because for the last fifteen years bands like Korn have been up there just banging out power chords and not really being flashy."

"It's a hard thing, being in a band with three other people. I don't care who you are: even if you're on top of the world, things get messed up, and feelings get hurt or something happens. It is like being married to three other people."

Richie Brown, once a member of Trivium, is happy that his friends are enjoying the fruits of their success. "I think that any band, anywhere, if they have good music and integrity and you know what you wanna do and you're 100% sure about it, and 100% confident about it, and you have the right support and motivation, and you're not making music for any of the wrong reasons – then you can achieve an amount of success," the guitarist says. "As long as you definitely believe in it, that's all really that matters. I can still call Matt's phone, and he'll answer it, and we're still friends. Everybody's still cool. I still see him at the grocery store and nothing's changed."

"I think we're very used to bands who seem to come with a game plan," says Mark Sutherland. "'We'll take a bit of this, a bit of that, stick it together, wear these clothes and we're guaranteed some attention, guaranteed to get in the *NME* or whatever'. A lot of bands really do think about that stuff now, before they go out and play gigs and before they make records. While Trivium have come up with a vision for the band, I don't think that they've done it just to sell records. It's just what they're into! And that does come across, you know, no-one would have those haircuts!"

"It's a consistent vision. A lot of bands spend a lot of time trying to please everybody, which isn't what being in a band's about. Certainly it's not what being in a heavy metal band's about. Trivium knows their niche, and they're sticking to it."

"It's amazing to see a mind that's so young, like Matt's, writing that kind of music," muses Alex Vieira – who so nearly was part of the explosion of success. "So complex, not only musically but also lyrically. It's amazing, it blows me away. A lot of people are raving about it; people ask me what I think about Matt as a musician. And I'm like, 'He's really good'. And everyone's like, 'That's it? *He's really good?*' 'Yeah, he's really good. But what scares me is *how good he's gonna be*. He's that good now; he's gonna be a *phenomenal* guitar player and overall musician in a few years.' Matt Heafy from Trivium: awesome musician and guitar player."

As for Stefan Luedicke, who signed the band to Lifeforce, he thinks the story is just beginning. "Metallica did something new with every record and you can see a lot of progression on every record, but their success did not come overnight," says the label boss. "It took them six albums before they reached the megastar status they have now, so there is still some time for Trivium. They are young and if they keep on working as hard as they do now I'm sure they can move their own status into *very* high regions." "It would be great if they could emulate Metallica," muses Colin Richardson, "this is album number two (sic) of hopefully a long career."

Rage Resteghini agrees. "I expect that this next record will triple or quadruple in terms of sales," he says. "I see them just getting bigger. Not only stylistically – which they've really become, stylised rock stars – but even physically. Travis is getting bigger in the shoulders and arms and Matt's filled out nicely, and vocally he's getting better. They're just going to continue to get better all the way around, as players, to being the rock stars that they so wanna be over the next several releases."

Gizz Butt, guitar hero and affable rock legend, sums it up. "They have a great team around them," he offers. "Travis is a killer drummer who plays mega catchy fills and beats. Their family and management, agency and record company are so entwined that it's a virtually flawless operation. They all support and love each other. Brian's a great dad. I've met Travis's family too. They're all really behind what's happening."

"I don't know how it happened," Matt Heafy concluded, "I don't know why it happened. I guess we're bringing the right kind of music that people want to hear right now. But as much as this is blowing up and we're becoming the biggest metal band in the UK, we're trying to make sure we have a good time while staying grounded and down to earth."

"Some people have nine-to-five jobs where they have to do something they hate all day, whereas for us we get to do something we love for an hour-and-a-half a day. And people like us for it."[187]

The understatement of the year: Matt, people *love* you for it.

One thing is for sure: Lake Brantley High will never see their like again. You will not read of this on the curriculum, but you may see the logo scrawled on toilet walls. You will hear them on the radio and watch them on TV. Maybe one day, these people will return to give talks and masterclasses on the instruments they play, and you might just see their faces at talent shows, checking out the new breed of bands they've helped to create more than anyone else.

These people are a musical group. They are called Trivium, and their crusade has only just begun.

And *that* is a fact.

selected Discography

Albums

Demo (2/03)
CD - Self-Released
To Burn The Eye / Requiem / Fugue / My Hatred /
The Storm / Sworn / Demon

Ember To Inferno (10/03)
CD - Lifeforce Records LF0040
Inception, The Bleeding Skies' / Pillars Of Serpents /
If I Could Collapse The Masses / Fugue (A Revelation) /
Requiem / Ember To Inferno / Ashes / To Burn The Eye /
Falling To Grey / My Hatred / When All Light Dies /
A View Of Burning Empires

Ember To Inferno – Japanese Release (12/03)
CD – Tokayuma Records
Inception, The Bleeding Skies' / Pillars Of Serpents /
If I Could Collapse The Masses / Fugue (A Revelation) /
Requiem / Ember To Inferno / Ashes / To Burn The Eye /
Falling To Grey / My Hatred / When All Light Dies /
A View Of Burning Empires / The Storm / Sworn

Ember To Inferno – Special Edition (6/05)
CD – Lifeforce Records LFR80402
Inception, The Bleeding Skies' / Pillars Of Serpents /
If I Could Collapse The Masses / Fugue (A Revelation) /
Requiem / Ember To Inferno / Ashes / To Burn The Eye /
Falling To Grey / My Hatred / When All Light Dies /
A View Of Burning Empires /
Blinding Tears Will Break The Skies / The Deceived / Demon
NOTES: Features different artwork to its original version, two
previously unreleased tracks, and 'Demon' from the 2003 Demo.

Ascendancy (3/05)
CD - Roadrunner Records RR82512
The End Of Everything / Rain /
Pull Harder On The Strings Of Your Martyr /
Drowned And Torn Asunder / Ascendancy /
A Gunshot To The Head Of Trepidation /
Like Light To The Flies / Dying In Your Arms / The Deceived /
Suffocating Sight / Departure / Declaration
NOTES: The Japanese version of 'Ascendancy' also features
'Washing Away Me In The Tides.' A 'clean' version was also released
sans explicit lyrics.

Ascendancy (Special Edition) (5/06)
CD – Roadrunner Records RR82518
Disc One (CD): The End Of Everything / Rain /
Pull Harder On The Strings Of Your Martyr /
Drowned And Torn Asunder / Ascendancy /
A Gunshot To The Head Of Trepidation /
Like Light To The Flies / Dying In Your Arms / The Deceived /
Suffocating Sight / Departure / Declaration /
Blinding Tears Will Break The Skies /
Washing Away Me In The Tides /
Master Of Puppets / Dying In Your Arms (Radio Mix)
Disc Two (DVD): Promo Videos - Like Light To The Flies /
Pull Harder On The Strings Of Your Martyr /
A Gunshot To The Head Of Trepidation /
Dying In Your Arms / Rain
Live at the London Astoria - 18/9/2005:
The End Of Everything (Intro) / Rain (Live) /
Dying In Your Arms (Live) / Like Light To The Flies (Live) /
A Gunshot To The Head Of Trepidation (Live) /
Pull Harder On The Strings Of Your Martyr (Live)

The Crusade (10/06)
CD – Roadrunner Records
Ignition / Detonation / Anthem (We Are the Fire) /
This World Can't Tear Us Apart / In Sadness We'll See Her /
Entrance Of The Conflagration / The Crusade / Synthetic /
Becoming the Dragon
*NOTES: Other tracks recorded at the sessions included
(some are working titles):*
Contempt Breeds Contamination / Vengeance /
To The Rats / Broken One / Gone Away (Far Away) /
Unrepentant / Contemporary Plague

singles

A Gunshot To The Head Of Trepidation
Download – Roadrunner Records

Like Light To The Flies
Download – Roadrunner Records

Pull Harder On The Strings Of Your Martyr
Download – Roadrunner Records

Dying In Your Arms
Download – Roadrunner Records

compilations

Kerrang! Field Of Screams (6/05)
CD – Kerrang! Exclusive Cover mount, Issue 1060
Track: Blinding Tears Will Break The Skies

Kerrang! Metallica: Remastered (4/06)
CD - Kerrang! Exclusive Cover mount, issue 1102
Track: Master Of Puppets

MTV2 Headbangers Ball Volume 2 (9/04)
CD - Roadrunner Records UPC: 016861825621
Track: Like Light To The Flies (Demo Version)

MTV2 Headbangers Ball: The Revenge (4/06)
CD - Roadrunner Records RR80602
Track: A Gunshot To The Head Of Trepidation

Roadrunner United: The All Star Sessions (10/05)
CD / DVD - Roadrunner Records RR81578
NOTES: Matt Heafy was one of four 'team captains' and wrote and played on the following:
In the Fire (also featuring Corey Beaulieu on lead guitar) /
Dawn Of A Golden Age / Blood & Flames /
I Don't Wanna Be (A Superhero)
Matt Heafy performed vocals on The End – a download single and video.

soundtracks

The Cave: Movie Soundtrack (8/05)
CD - Lakeshore Records LKS 33830
Track: Like Light To The Flies

Underworld: Evolution Soundtrack (2/06)
CD - Lakeshore Records LKS 33850
Track: Washing Away Me In The Tides

bootlegs

None as yet – but given the amount of gigs, rehearsals and pre-production demos that Trivium have recorded, no doubt some bootlegs will surface as time goes by. Of particular interest, however, if they surface, are the 2001 demos featuring the already-adept originals 'Pain' and 'Thrust', the 2002 effort that also includes 'Blitzkrieg' and 'Lake Of Fire' – and especially the 2003 Thanksgiving / pre-production demos for early versions of 'Ascendancy' tracks at Audiohammer. Matt told *Metal Maniacs* in July 2005 that he'd "found all our old demos and put them on my iPod – and they're fucking horrible."

Honest, at least.

other projects

Capharnaum – Fractured (2/05)
CD – Willowtip WTR027-2
Ingrained / Fractured / Perpetuate Catatonia / Machines / Icon Of Malice / Reins Of Humanity / The Scourge Trial / Refusal
NOTES: Features Matt Heafy on vocals, Jason Suecof on guitar and Trivium session bassist Mike Poggione.

Metal Militia – Perpetual State Of Aggression (4/03)
CD – Sonic Wave International ASIN: B00008VSD4
Darkest Days / Arbitrary / Perpetual State Of Aggression / Sick Of It All / Six String Suicide / Slave Of Darkness / The Feeder / Omnicide / Machines Of War / The Impending Holocaust
NOTES: Features Paolo Gregoletto on bass and vocals

videos

All available on 'Ascendancy – Special Edition' and for download from Trivium's official site:

Like Light To The Flies
Directed by Dale Resteghini for Raging Nation Films
Self-financed 2004 – original narrative unreleased, re-edited for release by Roadrunner 2005

Pull Harder On The Strings Of Your Martyr
Directed by Dale Resteghini for Raging Nation Films 2005

A Gunshot To The Head Of Trepidation
Directed by Dale Resteghini for Raging Nation Films 2005
Original narrative unreleased, re-edited for release by
Roadrunner 2005

Dying In Your Arms
Directed by Dale Resteghini for Raging Nation Films 2006

Rain
Directed by Paul Smith 2005

Roadrunner Roadrage (6/06)
DVD – Roadrunner Records RR09439
Tracks: A Gunshot To The Head Of Trepidation / Dying In
Your Arms
NOTES: Live DVD of the Roadrage tour.

Ozzfest 10th Anniversary DVD (11/05)
DVD / CD – Clear Channel Home Video CCVN0000109
*NOTES: Features Trivium's world-shattering performance of
'Like Light To The Flies' at 'Ozzfest day' at the Download festival,
June 11 2005, and a live CD with Trivium's 'A Gunshot To The
Head Of Trepidation'.*
Iron Maiden, unsurprisingly, do not appear on the DVD.

Total Guitar Meltdown DVD Vol 2 (2/06)
DVD (cover mount) – Total Guitar Magazine Issue 145
Matt & Corey give a masterclass in the art of shredding on this
cover mount DVD for the mag.

websites

www.trivium.org
Official Site with webmaster Brian at the helm...
guess who that might be?

www.roadrunnerrecords.co.uk/artists/trivium
Roadrunner's Official Trivium section, surprisingly enough.

www.lifeforcerecords.com/bands/18
Lifeforce Records' Official Trivium section.

**www.metalunderground.com/bands/
details.cfm?bandid=347**
Excellent metal site all round with news updated specific
to each band on its database regularly.

www.orlandometalawards.com
Matt Wagner's Orlando Metal Awards site. The clue is indeed
in the url.

www.trivium-u.com
Trivium Underground – an excellent unofficial site with lively
forums and plenty of media, rare artwork, video snippets and lots
to play with. If you only visit one site, this is the one to hit, yo.

www.purevolume.com/trivium
To listen to some of the tracks...

www.myspace.com/trivium
That site'll never catch on...

www.triviumslaves.com
Italian fan site.

www.gotrivium.com
Street team website dedicated to spreading the world about
the Floridians.

www.trivium-team.tk
Someone tell these youngsters that black text on a black
background is kinda tricky to read. Never watched Spinal Tap?
Still, some neat info there including interpretations of the lyrics
of 'Ascendancy' direct from Matt himself.

www.triviumworld.com
Fan site that features regular podcasts involving members of
Team Trivium and Suecof. Also see:
www.myspace.com/triviumworld

www.livejournal.com/community/triviumfans
Of interest for its browser skins and the like; not much
information to delve into though.

www.krakaos.org/trivium
Trivium Addicted – fan artwork, remixes, MP3s and all manner
of odd and good stuff.

www.blindingtears.co.uk
Japanese fan site run by the peerless Yuka Hirose.

trivium.blog28.fc2.com
Another Japanese site.

www.trivium.altervista.org
Italian site with English pages; live videos from Melkweg,
Download and more make it worth a scan.

www.trivium-fan.de.ms
German language site.

www.satansfishtank.com
The online site for the superb metal fanzine – massive
supporters of the band who gave them their first ever UK
cover.

Index of Articles
Referenced

Unless otherwise stated, all interviews are by the author during May, June and July 2006. Valuable publications during the writing of the book include *Metal Hammer, Rock Sound, Kerrang!, Metal Edge, Total Guitar, Guitar World, Drummer Magazine, Planet Loud, Pit Magazine, Satan's FishTank, Rhythm Magazine, Orlando Weekly, Power Play, Decibel Magazine, Bass Guitar Magazine, Revolver, Guitar One.*
Aside from those directly credited herewith, useful websites included *www.drownedinsound.com, www.metalunderground.com, www.wikipedia.com, www.uraniummusic.com* and the official websites *www.trivium.org* and *www.roadrunnerrecords.com* .

chapter 1
[1] Satan's FishTank Interview, Issue 16, Summer 2005
[2] Drummer Magazine Interview, June 2006
[3] www.metalupdate.com Interview, April 2005
[4] www.blastingzone.com Interview, June 2005
[5] Planet Loud Interview, May 2005
[6] Drummer Magazine Interview, June 2006
[7] Pit Magazine Interview, June 2006
[8] www.pitriff.com Interview, June 2004
[9] www.metalupdate.com Interview, April 2005
[10] Rhythm Magazine Interview, June 2006
[11] Metal Hammer Interview, March 2005
[12] Guitar World Interview, March 2005
[13] What Brad did next: "After Trivium I played guitar and didgeridoo in an instrumental band called Conjoined with Eyal Bar on drums, Matt Schuler on bass/sitar, and Sanghoon Shin on violin. We disbanded at the end of high school and I went to Ringling School of Art and Design where I studied computer animation for four years."

[14] Pit Magazine interview, April 2005
[15] www.blastingzone.com Interview, March 2006
[16] Rhythm Magazine Interview, June 2006
[17] Pit Magazine interview, April 2005
[18] Rock Sound Interview, August 2005

chapter 2

[19] www.brutalism.com Interview, October 2003
[20] www.quintessence.sh Interview, May 2003
[21] Ibid.
[22] Rhythm Magazine Interview, June 2006
[23] www.earache.com Interview, April 2005
[24] www.myspace.com/justinarcangel June 2006

chapter 3

[25] Orlando Music Weekly Interview, August 2004
[26] www.fourteeng.com Interview, August 2004
[27] www.metaljudgement.com Demo Review, June 2003
[28] www.hmas.org Demo Review, February 2003
[29] www.swedishmetal.net Demo Review, February 2003
[30] www.blistering.com Interview, October 2003
[31] www.kreemdesign.com News, May 2003
[32] Orlando Music Weekly Interview, August 2004
[33] www.metalupdate.com Interview, April 2005

chapter 4

[34] www.pitriff.com Interview, June 2004
[35] Ibid.
[36] www.unboundzine.com Interview, October 2003
[37] www.metalreviews.com Interview, December 2003
[38] Vinyl junkies often are to be found cackling to each other
about how 'real records sound warmer'. This is a dubious
phenomenon created and repeated ad nauseam by nostalgic
casualties of the 70s and 80s, supposedly due to the more
accurate reproduction of the master soundwaves that

analogue-based vinyl offers. In reality, the only people who can really tell the difference between a great vinyl disc and a top-end CD are confused, hairy, mole-like recording engineers who wear Syd Barrett-era Pink Floyd T-Shirts and have developed translucent skin from spending their whole lives in dark studios – and possibly certain breeds of dog.

[39] Guitar World Interview, May 2005

[40] www.metalreviews.com Interview, December 2003

[41] Barreing is a technique that involves making a chord shape with your left hand and moving the entire shape up and down the neck of the guitar to retain the same chord in different musical keys.

[42] Adrenaline Fanzine interview, November 2003

[43] Originally from Lifeforce Records' website, sourced from an August 2003 post, and the cache grabbed June 2006 by the author of this book

[44] Ibid.

[45] www.metalreviews.com Interview, December 2003

[46] Ibid.

[47] www.lordsofmetal.nl Interview, November 2003

[48] Ibid.

[49] www.metalreviews.com Interview, December 2003

[50] www.stereokiller.com Album Review, December 2003

[51] www.hmas.org Album Review, May 2004

[52] www.roughedge.com Album Review, February 2004

[53] www.metal-observer.com Album Review, December 2003. Apologies for my translation! Ich bin eine Dumbkopf.

[54] Unrestrained Magazine Album Review, Issue 23

chapter 5

[55] Decibel Magazine Interview, March 2005

[56] www.metalreviews.com Interview, December 2003

[57] Adrenaline Fanzine Interview, November 2003

[58] www.unboundzine.com Interview, October 2003

[59] www.roomthirteen.com Interview, May 2005

[60] www.roomthirteen.com Interview, May 2005

[61] www.pitriff.com Interview, June 2004

[62] Resteghini expanded: "It used to be, back in the day, that you having a demo was the key to getting to know an A&R and then getting a showcase for them. And then it was the Electronic Press Kit. And that's all gone by the wayside. Now really A&Rs don't exist any more; there used to be a staff of 20 on a major label and now there's like two and a half, and then on the indies anybody who sees anything might be able to bring it to the table – but if there's 10 or 15 projects sitting on somebody's desk who can sign somebody, and they're all about the same level, maybe one's a little bit better, the one that has a killer visual is 99% of the time gonna be the band that's gonna get signed. Not only a) it's something the label doesn't have to spend money on, but b) it gets them the most play right away because they can start sending it out via the web, via the video stations; it lets them show the world what this band is. They don't have to do research, they don't have to go and spend money on marketing it, and go through the whole process. That's what's really starting to happen, and what happened with Trivium."

[63] Roadrunner press release, as posted on http://www.roadrunnerrecords.co.uk/artists/Trivium/index.aspx?PageNum=12 April, 2004

[64] Orlando Music Weekly Interview, August 2004

[65] Kerrang! Interview, July 2005

[66] Rock Sound Interview, August 2005

[67] www.uraniummusic.com Interview, April 2004.

[68] www.metalupdate.com Interview, April 2005

[69] Kerrang! Interview, July 2005

[70] Ibid.

[71] Ibid.

[72] www.uraniummusic.com Interview, April 2004

[73] Ibid.

chapter 6

[74] www.fourteeng.com Interview, August 2004

[75] www.uraniummusic.com Interview, May 2004

[76] www.pitriff.com Interview, June 2004

[77] www.daredevil.de Live Review, May 2004

[78] www.icedearth.com News, June 2004

[79] www.uraniummusic.com Interview, May 2004

[80] Ibid.

[81] www.fourteeng.com Interview, August 2004

[82] Poggione was told by Matt that Brent left the band because he did not want to commit to such a vigorous touring schedule and did not want to be away from his girlfriend.

[83] Metal to the core, Mike Poggione elaborates on possible reasons he didn't fit in. "I remember a show in Jersey - we played a great set that time but there were like four guys in front of me that kept screaming 'Fuck Trivium – you suck' for half our set. Finally, I got fed up with all the verbal taunts and after a song I went off on them threatening them, telling them I'd beat them to a pulp and bash them all here in front of everyone at the show (1000 plus crowd). After this happened the place went nuts and the crowd seemed to love my confrontation with the four fans. I have that on tape - I was really proud to be a part of Trivium and I wasn't gonna take that shit from those losers in the crowd. I remember [some of the] crew being upset that I acted like that – trying to fight some shit talkers in my face as I played. I told them, 'This is metal, what do you expect from me, huh?' To this day I don't understand why. This is metal, not some school dance where you don't want to step on other's shoes."

[84] www.roadrunnerrecords.co.uk News, August 2004

[85] Orlando Weekly 2004 Awards, July 2004 – as quoted on www.roadrunnerrecords.co.uk News, July 2004

[86] Bass Guitar Magazine Interview, July/August 2006

[87] Ibid.

[88] www.thegreatnothing.com Interview, 2005

[89] The set-list for the tour intriguingly comprised new material – at the Chicago date the band hammered through mostly new tracks: 'Rain' / 'Drowned And Torn Asunder' / 'Pull Harder On The Strings of Your Martyr' / 'Suffocating Sight' / 'Like Light To Flies' were debuted, probably with an eye on tweaking and perfecting them for the forthcoming sessions for their new album. Only 'Pillars Of Serpents' had survived to the live arena from the 'Ember To Inferno' LP. Setlist sourced from www.fourteeng.net/Roadrage.html

[90] www.roadrunnerrecords.co.uk News, August 2004

[91] Revolver Interview, February 2005

[92] Decibel Magazine Interview, December 2005

[93] Guitar World Interview, March 2005

[94] www.pitriff.com Interview, 2004

[95] www.live4metal.com Live Review, August 2004

[96] And what is more, you'll be a man, my son.

[97] Carve Magazine Interview, April 2005

[98] www.blastingzone.com Interview, June 2005

[99] That the band had a deal with a legendary international metal record label rather than an enthusiastic ground-level European imprint may have made the decision slightly easier than it had been for Vieira and Moore – but them's the breaks, babydoll.

chapter 7

[100] Or the fifteenth, given the band's constant line-up reshuffles...

[101] Metal Edge Interview, March 2005

[102] www.roadrunnerrecords.co.uk News, September 2004

[103] www.fourteeng.com Interview, April 2005

[104] This is also in part due to the way the guitars are tuned, in Trivium's case usually drop D. On a standard tuning, the lowest string on a guitar is E, and dropping this note to D tuning makes the overall sound balance lower and more

muscular sounding. It creates an effect many metal bands have used over the years because the general tone of the chords and therefore the music itself is changed considerably. Initially, for the *Ascendancy* sessions, Trivium had tuned down to D flat, something quickly abandoned in favour of drop D as going too low can make the sound muddier. The band Slayer often tune all the way down to drop B, hence the low-end rumble of sphincter-loosening doom that is their signature. Who needs a bass player anyway? There are many different tunings that can be used: slide Blues guitars are sometimes tuned to an open D minor chord, and Led Zep's Jimmy Page also used his own unique tuning a lot of the time.

[105] Guitar One Magazine Interview, February 2005

[106] Guitar World Interview, May 2005

[107] Power Play Interview, March 2005

[108] Scratch Magazine Interview, May 2005

[109] Outburn Magazine Interview, April 2005

[110] www.blastingzone.com Interview, June 2005

[111] Pit Magazine Interview, April 2005

[112] Metal Edge Interview, March 2005

[113] www.fourteeng.com Interview, April 2005

[114] www.metalforce.com Interview, May 2005

[115] Pit Magazine Interview, April 2005

[116] Power Play Interview, March 2005

[117] www.foundrymusic.com Interview, February 2005

[118] Chips are made from potatoes, cut to finger length and girth, deep fried for not quite long enough, and eaten hot directly from newspapers, possibly along with a battered sausage and a pickled egg. That is what chips are. What chips are not are those cold, thin, crispy things that you buy in colourful plastic bags from newsagents. The crispy things that come in a multitude of flavours including cheese 'n' onion, ready salted and hedgehog. Those 'crispy' things are called crisps. Sayin'?

chapter 8

[119] New York Metro Interview, January 2005

[120] www.metalreview.com Live Review, January 2005

[121] www.rockreview.co.uk Interview, March 2006

[122] Decibel Magazine Live Review, March 2005

[123] Remember that little talk we had in the last chapter? Good.

[124] The setlist for the tour was 'Rain' /
'Drowned And Torn Asunder' / 'Suffocating Sight' /
'Pull Harder On The Strings Of Your Martyr' /
'A Gunshot To The Head Of Trepidation' /
'Ascendancy' and 'Like Light To The Flies'

[125] www.themetalforge.com Interview, May 2005

[126] www.montagpress.com Interview, June 2005

[127] www.metalrage.com Album Review, February 2005

[128] Hard Beat Magazine Album Review, February 2005

[129] www.ecromper.com Album Review, Feburary 2005

[130] www.live4metal.com Album Review, February 2005

[131] www.lordsofmetal.nl Album Review, March 2005

[132] www.breakingcustom.com Album Review, February 2005

[133] www.roughedge.com Interview, March 2005

[134] www.trivium.org News, March 2005

[135] www.roughedge.com Interview, March 2005

[136] Crave Magazine Interview, March 2005

[137] www.roughedge.com Interview, March 2005

[138] www.metalunderground.com Interview, March 2005

[139] Kerrang! Live Review, March 2005

[140] www.trivium.org News, March 2005

[141] Kerrang! Album Review, March 12 2005

[142] Power Play Album Review, March 2005

[143] Metal Hammer Album Review, March 2005

[144] Rock Sound Album Review, April 2005

[145] www.metaluk.com Interview, May 2005

[146] Ibid.

chapter 9

147 www.metal.4Qradio.com Interview, May 2005

148 www.ultimatemetal.com/forum Interview, May 2005

149 Ibid.

150 www.metalupdate.com Interview, April 2005

151 www.ultimatemetal.com Live Review, May 2005

152 Satan's FishTank Live Review, Issue 16, Summer 2005

153 www.trivium.org News, May 2005

154 www.mtv.com News, May 30, 2005

155 www.meltrage.com Interview, May 2005

156 Decibel Magazine Interview, June 2005

157 www.ozzfest.com News, June 2005

chapter 10

158 Kerrang! Magazine Live Review, June 2005

159 Kerrang! Magazine Interview, July 2005

160 www.azcentral.com Live Review, August 2005

161 Trivium's setlist for Ozzfest was 'Rain' / 'Ascendancy' /
    'A Gunshot To The Head Of Trepidation' / 'Pull Harder On
    The Strings Of Your Martyr' / 'Like Light To The Flies'

162 An online vote taken for the video that the participants rated
    the highest. Nevermore pulled 40% for their video, 'Final
    Product'; Trivium's 'Pull Harder' gathering 36%

163 Satan's FishTank Interview, Issue 17, Autumn 2005

164 Metal Hammer Interview, October 2005

165 Satan's FishTank Interview, Issue 17, Autumn 2005

166 www.rockontheweb.co.uk Interview, December 2005

167 www.rockreview.co.uk Interview, March 2006

168 The set for the tour was 'Rain' /
    'Drowned And Torn Asunder' / 'The Deceived' /
    'Suffocating Sight' / 'Ascendancy' / 'Like Light To The Flies' /
    'A Gunshot To The Head Of Trepidation'
    and 'Pull Harder On The Strings Of Your Martyr'

169 www.trivium.org News, October 2005

chapter 11

[170] The set for the tour: Rain' / 'Drowned And Torn Asunder' /
'Like Light To The Flies'/ 'Suffocating Sight /
'The Deceived' / 'Declaration' /
'A Gunshot To The Head Of Trepidation' and
'Pull Harder On The Strings Of Your Martyr'

[171] www.themegalith.com Live Review, November 22, 2005

[172] www.maximummetal.com Interview, December 2005

[173] 'Football' is a team game beloved by billions worldwide,
where the aim is to kick a round ball between two sticks and
UNDER a crossbar, thus scoring a point. That's kicking,
with your feet. That's why it's called 'football', a word that's
derived from 'foot' and 'ball'. That odd version of rugby
played mostly by American guys in crash helmets -
competing in leagues with teams called things like the
'Charlton Heston Dividers', 'East Bay Ray' and suchlike –
largely involves throwing and catching an oval-shaped, air-
filled bladder – which semantically-speaking doesn't actually
count as a ball as it's not spherical. That you sometimes kick
said 'ball' OVER the crossbar is of secondary importance.
I'm glad we're able to have these little chats.

[174] Total Guitar Interview, January 2006

[175] www.metalrage.com Interview, January 2006

[176] www.trivium.org News, January 2006

[177] www.adequacy.net Live Review, February 2006

[178] Metal Hammer Interview, January 2006

[179] The tracks were 'Dying In Your Arms' /
'Pull Harder On The Strings Of Your Martyr', /
'A Gunshot To The Head Of Trepidation' and
'Like Light To The Flies'

[180] As quoted on www.roadrunner.com News, March 2006

[181] www.trivium.org News, March 2006

[182] www.trivium.org News, March 2006

[183] www.quintessence.com Interview, March 2006

[184] Satan's FishTank Interview, Issue 19

[185] Guitar World Interview, February 2006
[186] Total Guitar Interview, January 2006
[187] Play Music Interview, April 2006

ALSO AVAILABLE FROM
independent music press...

MY CHEMICAL ROMANCE:
SOMETHING INCREDIBLE THIS WAY COMES
by Paul Stenning

New Jersey band My Chemical Romance have taken the music underground by storm since their incendiary debut album in 2002. Within weeks of its release, major labels across the globe were frantically pulling out their cheque-books in an attempt to capture what is widely regarded as the world's next stadium-selling rock band in the vein of Metallica, Foo Fighters and Green Day. Their biting lyrics, beautiful visuals and relentless touring schedules have ensured that MCR have already captured the hearts and minds of the I-Pod generation – the year 2006 will see them promoted to the very upper echelons of rock music's giants.

This is the very first book to tell their tale, from the humble New Jersey beginnings, setting them in the context of the dormant US rock scene, through to their breakthrough live shows and meteoric success in 2004 and 2005 that sees them perched on the cusp of being a multi-million-selling global force. Mixing metal with ballads, rock with pop, MCR are the next big band. This book tells you how this bunch of introverted high school friends achieved their dream.

ISBN 0 9549704 5 4   176 Pages   Paperback, 8pp colour pics   £8.99   World Rights

For more information please visit www.impbooks.com

SYSTEM OF A DOWN:
RIGHT HERE IN HOLLYWOOD
by Ben Myers

Spewed forth from the loins of mid-90s southern California, System Of A
Down have evolved from a cult band whose demo tapes swapped hands
voraciously on the metal underground to one of the world's biggest bands.
Relentless early gigging spread a word-of-mouth hype around them that
soon elicited major label interest and the gold-selling eponymous debut
album. Despite their ultra-hard music and dark undertones, SOAD have
always managed to break out of the underground. Show-stealing support
slots with Ozzy Osbourne and Slayer propelled the band to new heights, but
it was their second album, the seminal Toxicity, that turned SOAD from an
underground phenomenon into a mainstream smash. By the end of 2005 –
with their globally acclaimed hit album Mesmerize under their belts – SOAD
had shifted in excess of 25 million albums. With exclusive new interviews
with the band and major players involved in their story, Ben Myers' book will
be the first and the definitive account of this remarkable group.

ISBN 0 9549704 6 2 208 Pages Paperback, 8pp b/w pics £12.99 World Rights

For more information please visit www.impbooks.com

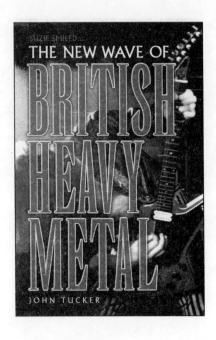

SUZIE SMILED:
THE NEW WAVE OF BRITISH HEAVY METAL
by John Tucker

This book tells the definitive and complete history of the NWOBHM, from its formation during the late Seventies, through its numerous peaks and troughs in the Eighties and on to its current status as one of rock music's most influential genres. The most famous exponents of this New Wave are stadium-selling acts such as Motorhead, Def Leppard and the currently-enormous-again Iron Maiden, but there are also scores of other acts who have been selling millions of records to the movement's enormous and fanatical fanbase for years.

Suzie Smiled... The NWOBHM describes, in those bands' own words, what it was like to be writing and playing heavy metal in the post-punk era and sets the music in the bleak social context of the time.

Through a mixture of exclusive new interviews, contemporary articles and many unpublished photographs, Suzie Smiled... lets the musicians tell the entire story in their own words, including how some of the greatest heavy metal songs ever written were created.

*ISBN 0 9549704 7 0   256 Pages Paperback, 20pp b/w pics £12.99 **World Rights***

For more information please visit www.impbooks.com

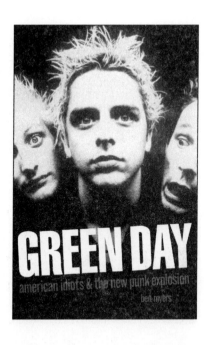

GREEN DAY: AMERICAN IDIOTS AND
THE NEW PUNK EXPLOSION
by Ben Myers

The world's first and only full biography of Green Day. Self-confessed latch-
key kids from small blue-collar Californian towns, Green Day have gone on
to sell 50 million albums and single-handedly redefine the punk and rock
genre for an entire generation. Inspired by both the energy of British punk
bands as well as cult American groups, Green Day gigged relentlessly across
the US underground before eventually signing to Warners and releasing their
1994 major label debut *Dookie*, which was a 10-million-selling worldwide hit
album. With the arrival of Green Day, suddenly music was dumb, fun, upbeat
and colourful again. Many now credit the band with saving rock from the
hands of a hundred grunge-lite acts. In 2004 Green Day reached a career
pinnacle with the concept album *American Idiot*, a sophisticated
commentary on modern life - not least their dissatisfaction with their
president. Myers is an authority on punk and hardcore and in this
unauthorised book charts the band members' difficult childhoods and their
rise to success, speaking to key members of the punk underground and
music industry figures along the way.

ISBN 0 9539942 9 5 208 Pages Paperback, 8pp b/w pics £12.99 World Rights

For more information please visit www.impbooks.com

MUSE: INSIDE THE MUSCLE MUSEUM
by Ben Myers

The first and only biography of one of the most innovative and successful rock bands of recent years. Formed in the mid-1990s in a sleepy sea-side Devonshire town, Muse comprises teenage friends Matt Bellamy, Chris Wolstenholme and Dominic Howard. 2001's *Origin Of Symmetry* album spawned Top 10 hits such as 'Plug-In Baby' and a unique version of Nina Simone's classic, 'Feeling Good'. Their third album, *Absolution*, entered the UK charts at Number 1 in October 2003 – by then, all the signs were there that Muse were on the verge of becoming one of the biggest bands of the new century. Throughout 2004, they won over countless new fans at festivals, including a now-famous headline slot at Glastonbury, which preceded a two-night sell-out of the cavernous Earl's Court and a Brit Award for 'Best Live Act' in early 2005. This book tells that full story right from their inception and includes interviews conducted both with the band and those who have witnessed their climb to the top - a position they show no sign of relinquishing any time soon.

ISBN 0 9539942 6 0 208 Pages Paperback, 8pp b/w pics £12.99 World Rights

For more information please visit www.impbooks.com

DAVE GROHL: FOO FIGHTERS, NIRVANA AND OTHER MISADVENTURES
by Martin James

The first biography of one of modern rock's most influential figures. Emerging from the morass of suicide and potent musical legacy that was Nirvana, Foo Fighters established themselves - against all odds - as one of the most popular rock bands in the world. Deflecting early critical disdain, Dave Grohl has single-handedly reinvented himself and cemented his place in the rock pantheon. This is his story, from his pre-Nirvana days in hardcore band Scream to his current festival-conquering status as a Grammy-winning, platinum-selling grunge legend reborn. Martin James once found himself watching the Prodigy backstage with Grohl, both clambering up a lighting rig to share a better view. With this in-depth book, he pieces together the life story of one of the most remarkable, enigmatic and yet amenable stars in recent music history.

ISBN 0 9539942 4 4 208 Pages Paperback, b/w pics £12.99 World Rights

For more information please visit www.impbooks.com

Visit our website at **www.impbooks.com**
for more information on our full list of titles including
books on *System of a Down, Dave Grohl, Muse,*
My Chemical Romance, The Killers, The Streets,
Green Day, The Prodigy and many more.